DO-IT-YOURSELF
INVESTMENT ANALYSIS

Practical Guide to
Life Cycle, Fundamental and Technical Analyses

DO-IT-YOURSELF
INVESTMENT ANALYSIS

Practical Guide to
Life Cycle, Fundamental and Technical Analyses

James Burgauer

International Publishing Corporation
Chicago

Library of Congress Catalog Card Number: 89-83752

ISBN Number: 0-942641-24-8

Printed in the United State of America
10 9 8 7 6 5 4 3 2 1

This publication is designed to provide accurate and authoritative information in regard to the subject matter covered. However, it is sold with the understanding that the publisher is not engaged in rendering legal or professional investment services. If legal advice or other expert assistance is required, a competent professional should be retained.

CONTENTS

PREFACE

Thousands of books have been written on the subject of investing, yet very few of them can be considered to be of reference quality. Fewer still tell where to get information or how to use it to make sound investment decisions.

Do-It-Yourself Investment Analysis is designed to do just that. The book provides sufficient background to understand and apply concepts and phraseology used by investment professionals and the investment community in general. Key information and techniques for evaluating current investment opinions, analyzing prospective investments, and executing profitable trades are included.

Chapter 1, "Life Cycle Analysis," discusses the importance of analyzing a business life cycle and how a company's investment characteristics relate to its current stage of development. The chapter begins with a discussion on the uses of investment capital, highlighting both how and why companies raise money; proceeds to the changes a company will undergo as it grows from a private company to an industry force; and concludes with a set of corollaries that investors should keep in mind as they evaluate various investment opportunities.

Chapter 2, "Fundamental Analysis," begins with an explanation of where various fundamental data can be found and follows with twenty-five fundamental analysis ratios most frequently used in analyzing a company. Each equation term is defined and related to the ratio's specific use. To facilitate a working understanding of the formulas, an example is illustrated using data obtained from the Sara Lee Corporation. The chapter concludes with an overall analysis, utilizing the Du Pont analysis, which illustrates the relationship between all fundamental ratios and how each one impacts the organization as well as the shareholder.

Chapter 3, "Fundamental Analysis and Market Valuation," discusses the ratios used to compare company factors with those of the market. These ratios are then applied to a simple "stock screening and evaluation" worksheet which can be used to evaluate a security against the market and industry and to determine the intrinsic value of the stock. This chapter concludes with the valuation of the Sara Lee Corporation and a brief discussion of market risk, beta.

Chapter 4, "Technical Analysis," first gives an overview of the various data technicians use to determine what future price and trading patterns will be. It then moves on to a comprehensive, yet understandable, course on Technical Analysis—charts and trends, gaps, reversal patterns, and market theories. It also covers the role computers have played in gathering and analyzing technical information, concluding with a discussion of software and on-line database services available to individual investors.

Chapter 5, "Portfolio Performance Benchmarks," examines how analysts and individuals use averages and indices as benchmarks to gauge the overall performance of the markets and personal investment portfolios. The differences between the most popular averages and indices and how they are calculated are thoroughly covered.

To further assist do-it-yourself analysis, this book presents a number of illustrations, an Appendix of Sources of Information, and a detailed Glossary.

All in all, a lot of work has gone into compiling the information in this book. Most of the data that you will find in *Do-It-Yourself Investment Analysis* exists nowhere else—it is the product of primary research. Special thanks to John Bajkowski, financial analyst with the American Association of Individual Investors. John's contributions make this book a more complete do-it-yourself investment analysis guide.

Finally, I dedicate this book to my daughter, Janene, who learned very quickly in life which book in daddy's library ought to be her favorite.

1 / LIFE CYCLE ANALYSIS

OVERVIEW

Businesses and industries evolve through stages of development called the business life cycle. The life cycle of a business can be compared to the development of human life—growth is rapid in the early stages of development and tapers off as adulthood approaches. This is followed by a long period of maturity after which some decline occurs. For a business, each stage of development indicates its growth potential as well as its need for money to finance this growth. Throughout its entire life cycle, a business needs capital. As the business grows, more and more capital is needed for property and equipment, inventory, and working cash. As the business and its capital needs grow, overall funding requirements change. And as they change, so do the risks associated with the capital and the sources from which this capital can be obtained.

All too often investors forget that the money they have invested *is* this capital. This "paper" represents bricks and mortar in some town where employees come to work, produce goods and services, and collect their paychecks. Shares of stock and bonds comprise capital being used to create more capital. That is what the system of capitalism is all about.

A basic tenet of this system is that investment capital needs to be rewarded by the payment of some rate of return. Additionally, the higher the risk an investment represents, the higher the rate of return necessary to attract capital into the investment. Simply stated, there exists a trade-off between risk and reward that dictates "added risk requires added reward." Table 1.1 illustrates the typical levels of risk associated with the different stages of business or industry development.

Keeping in mind that the life cycle of a business in analogous to the development of a human, review Table 1.2, which shows a typical classification of the human life cycle and the risk preferences associated with those stages.

Table 1.1. Typical risk levels of a business life cycle

Stage	Risk Level
Development	High
Aggressive Growth	High
Growth	Medium
Mature	Low

Prior to dealing in securities, investors need to assess personal investment goals and determine how much risk can be assumed. During early and mid-career, individuals are gathering wealth. This is best done with aggressive growth and growth. By late career, looking more to preserve wealth, individuals utilize growth and mature firms. By retirement, investors may look to mature firms for

Table 1.2. Human life cycle and risk preferences

Life Cycle	Risk Preference
Early Career	High
Mid-Career	High
Late Career	Medium
Retirement	Low

dividend cash flow. Prudent investors not only select securities that are appropriate to their individual needs, but they also diversify the securities in their portfolios, periodically and systematically evaluate their holdings, and recompose their portfolios as personal characteristics and objectives change.

Following is a brief discussion of the risk and return characteristics of debt and equity investments. This is then followed by a discussion showing how the analysis of a business life cycle can be used effectively to provide information about specific firms in order to make investment decisions based on pre-determined investment goals. Remember, added reward requires added risk.

DEBT AND EQUITY INVESTMENT CHARACTERISTICS

In its most simplistic form, the capital market can be broken down into two broad classifications—debt and equity. Debt represents the money borrowed by the business; equity represents the ownership interest. When capital is borrowed, a contract is drawn up specifying how much interest should be paid and when the borrowed money should be repaid. Legally, debt takes precedence over equity. Debt interest payments must be made before any excess capital can be distributed to equityholders in the form of dividends. Should the business fail, holders of debt will be paid back before equityholders. For these reasons, debt securities are considered to be safer than equities. And, given the greater assurances debtholders have that they will receive their original capital back at some stated point in the future, debtholders generally require lower rates of returns on their investments than do equityholders.

Equity securities, generally thought of as common stock, carry virtually no assurances about the rate of return the investor will receive, nor any assurance about repayment of principal. From the investor's viewpoint, the risks associated with equities are generally thought to be much higher than those associated with debt. Therefore, the rate of return required on equity capital is higher than that of debt.

The rate of return on debt, like that of equity, is the total return generated from both cash flow and appreciation. Cash flow, in the case of debt, is determined by market forces at the time the company wishes to raise capital. It is set at a fixed rate, called *interest*. Furthermore, debt securities mature at par, meaning they return a *stated* amount of capital. Thus, regardless of the price the investor pays for the debt security, the total return on the investment is calculable. Assuming the issuer doesn't default on the debt, it offers no potential for either more or less return than this calculated rate.

On the other hand, cash flow of equities (*dividends*) is determined by the board of directors of the company and is subject to change without notice. Appreciation is determined by the profit generated when the investment is sold. In a perfect world, appreciation is a function of the earnings of the company. It is incalculable at the time the investment is made, though analysts and investors attempt to estimate the potential for it in order to evaluate a fair price for an equity as well as its rate of return. In the event this rate of return is never achieved, investors merely dismiss it as one of the risks of investing.

The chance for equityholders to share in the growth of a business offers investors financial opportunities that debt instruments do not. The uncertainty of equity returns, however, requires that they be carefully analyzed before any money is invested. Life cycle analysis provides an initial framework within which to examine companies and select those that fit into investment objectives and personal circumstances.

THE BUSINESS LIFE CYCLE

Equity securities are generally categorized based on where a business is within its life cycle when the capital is invested. The younger the firm, the riskier its securities are assumed to be, and the higher the rate of return required to attract investment in those securities. The more mature the firm, the less risk associated with it, and the lower the rate of return required to attract investment capital.

Combining this knowledge with the fact that it is management's express responsibility to maximize shareholder wealth, we can presume that if the firm can reinvest money at a rate of return higher than its shareholders are able to, then it is in the best interest of the shareholders for the firm to retain this excess cash and invest it accordingly. Younger firms with exceptional growth prospects tend to do this, reinvesting their excess funds rather than paying them out. Older firms with less exceptional prospects for growth or with too much cash flow to reinvest typically pay the funds out as dividends.

The decline in earnings growth rate as dividends increase is shown in Figure 1.1. In essence, this is the basis for the inverse relationship between a company's growth prospects and its dividend yield; companies with higher prospects for growth typically have lower dividend yields because they tend to retain cash to fund a higher rate of growth.

As a firm continues to grow and mature, management eventually runs out of investment opportunities within the confines of the company to earn rates of return higher than its shareholders can earn elsewhere. Obliged to properly manage this excess cash flow, firms often buy back their own shares, buy the shares of other more aggressive companies, or pay increasingly larger cash distributions to shareholders.

In the business life cycle, businesses fall into four broad stages—*development, aggressive growth, growth,* and *mature*—which

Figure 1.1. Earnings growth rate and dividend yield

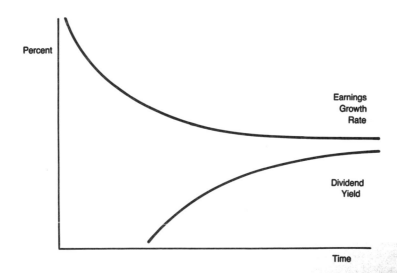

describe a company's phase of maturity and help determine the risk level associated with its shares and the company's ability to raise capital. An abstract of time in the business life cycle in which each phase is most common is shown in Figure 1.2.

Figure 1.2. Phases in the business life cycle

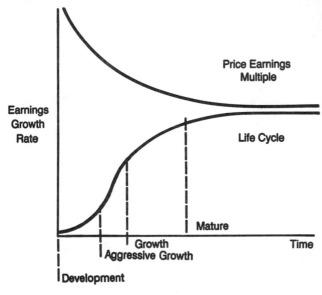

Development Stage

At the beginning of the development stage, start-up or seed money is needed to get the business going. Generally securities of this stage are thought to be the riskiest of all types of equity investments because many start-up companies fail soon after inception. Usually seed money comes directly from the people who created the business and plan to run it on a day-to-day basis.

As the company develops, additional funds are needed to pay for expansion. This usually forces a firm to seek venture capital. Though sometimes these crucial funds can be generated internally, often they must be obtained through a private placement—from a wealthy individual or local financier, or a venture capitalist. Dozens of firms billing themselves as venture capitalists will not only finance a small concern but lend professional expertise to the existing organization. In return for their investment, venture capitalists usually require ownership of a large percentage of the company, representation on the board of directors, and positions as officers within the company.

Many venture capitalist organizations are sponsored by corporate giants; some are built around the fortunes of private individuals or closely held brokerage concerns; others are organized as publicly registered investment companies, or mutual funds. In all cases significant risk exists for capital invested in this fashion, and the average investor predisposed to making such investments is advised that the safest way to do so is through a mutual fund specializing in venture capital.

Aggressive Growth Stage

Once a company has generated some degree of stability, it enters a phase of aggressive growth typically financed by an initial public offering (IPO). With an IPO, a company's ownership is taken out of the private hands of those who started the company and financed it through a venture capitalist. Both parties stand to make a high return for their initial investment as their shares are sold to the public through the various exchanges or the over-the-counter market. In an IPO, a brokerage firm evaluates the company vis-a-vis the potential sales success of its securities to clientele and determines whether the brokerage firm can raise the capital the company requires. Basically, only two groups of brokerage firms sponsor IPOs. The first is a major brokerage house, as represented by a national or large regional firm. The second is the penny stock house, usually a small, one- or two-office firm with a high concentration of brokers in states having less stringent securities laws.

In general IPOs come in only two varieties: best-efforts offerings and underwritings. In a *best-efforts offering*, the brokerage firm makes no guarantee to sell any of the shares offered by the firm wishing to go public, committing only to making its best efforts in soliciting sales of the shares. In an *underwriting*, the brokerage firm guarantees that all shares will be sold; in essence, buying the entire offering for its own account and in turn reselling the shares to its clients. Generally, the better known a company is the better the chance it has to command an underwriting.

Because the large national or regional brokerage firms tend to raise capital through underwritings, they consider only the most prestigious, well-established businesses wishing to go public. The primary reason is that the large brokerage firms refuse to accept the market risks of being "stuck" holding any unsold shares. Further, the high costs of due diligence and national promotion limit the major brokerage firms to only the largest public offerings that will generate sufficient underwriting fees to cover their costs. Unfortunately, this forces the smaller, lesser-known firms—or firms not wishing to raise enormous amounts of capital—to migrate toward the penny stock brokerage firms who represent the only other reasonable alternative for publicly raising capital.

Despite common misconceptions that firms using penny stock brokerage firms are somehow a greater risk, are of lower quality, or have less integrity than firms going public through a major brokerage house, to judge them on this basis alone would be grossly unfair. Also, to suggest that a security brought to market by a major brokerage house automatically represents a good value at a fair price would be a misjudgment. To be very pragmatic, firms wishing to go public are out to raise the most money possible by giving up the fewest shares. By the same token, the brokerage firm taking them public is out to maximize its profit on the transaction as well, and the investors are the people who pay for it. Good and bad values arise through both types of underwritings. The best advice to investors is to use good judgment, complete the necessary homework, and beware the risks associated with this type of investing.

With the new capital raised from the IPO, the firm expands its scope of operations. If the firm is successful in these endeavors, earnings will expand rapidly. Investors, noting this, will most likely bid up the price of the shares, expanding the company's price-earnings multiple. Further increases in earnings will translate into still higher prices for the stock; and as long as the growth rate continues, so presumably will the stock's price appreciation. This scenario continues until the company's growth rate eventually begins to slow. This then causes a moderate decline in the price-earnings multiple investors are willing to apply to the shares, and the company's stock price may begin to stagnate or even decline. More aggressive investors, noting this, may liquidate their holdings, putting further downward pressure on the price of the stock. However, aggressive growth stocks bought and sold in a timely fashion can translate into enormous gains for an aggressive growth-oriented investor. But investing in this fashion may require strong financial resources and very active portfolio management. Individuals investing in aggressive growth companies are concerned with capital appreciation. Because these shares pay little, if any, cash dividends, investors receive their return through an increase in a stock's price.

Growth Stage

Having passed the aggressive growth phase, a young company begins to settle into a slightly more predictable pattern—the growth phase of its life cycle. The firm often devotes significantly more resources to research and development, with the specific intention of staying one step ahead of its competition.

Adopting this strategy may generate some new product or process that once again places the company in a phase of aggressive growth. If it doesn't, management may try to acquire a younger, more aggressive firm to rekindle the company's former, more aggressive posture, or it may settle back, choosing to run the company in a less-aggressive fashion. In the latter case, the company typically releases several new or related products in an effort to expand its client base while solidifying ties with its existing accounts. Earnings growth will continue to slow, and investors will begin to stabilize the price-earnings multiple that they apply to the company's earnings, typically assigning lower multiples than they did during the company's aggressive growth phase. At this point the company often begins to pay modest cash dividends as management attempts to ingratiate itself with the investment community. Though the firm may have several years of excellent growth left, these actions typically signal the beginning of the transition into the next phase of a company's life cycle, replete with still lower earnings growth rates and price-earnings multiples.

Given proper timing, investments in companies at this point in their life cycles can be very profitable. The savvy investor, however, also knows that the transition from aggressive growth to growth, and from growth to maturity, can create a very rocky road for a company's stock price. Investors should certainly consider all risks inherent in poorly timed investments of this nature. Individuals investing in companies at this stage of their life cycles are still interested in capital appreciation, but also want some income in the form of cash dividends.

Mature Stage

In the mature phase of its life cycle, a company's products will become even more established in the marketplace. Oftentimes aging products are replaced by reworked ones sporting minor improvements and billed as "new and improved," rather than entirely new products developed through updated technology. Sales continue to generate excess cash flow, which is used to develop new markets, streamline internal operations, and fund higher dividend payouts. Earnings growth may slow further, though in cardinal numbers earnings will most likely be at record levels for the firm.

Perceiving this higher degree of stability, investors come to look on the shares as situations with a reasonable degree of predictability of earnings growth and a reasonable level of dividend yield. Management often perceives this shift in investor emphasis and may even attempt to substantiate this perception by adopting a philosophy of moderate dividend increases when they can be supported by earnings advances. Sporting both higher stability and higher yield, investments in this type of company can also be very profitable.

Having "made it," management may choose to embark on one of many routes to further enhance the company's future. For instance, if the industry has become either oligopolistic or highly regulated, management is likely to settle back and attempt to manipulate the marketplace to achieve some long-term profit targets without upsetting too many applecarts. Or, if the industry is still relatively competitive, management may attempt to increase market share through the acquisition of other companies within the industry—i.e., establish buying growth. If the industry is still extremely competitive or if the market potential for the company's product lines is expected to decline, management may choose to diversify the company's interests by acquiring firms in unrelated industries, thus molding the company into a conglomerate. Mature companies appeal more to investors, such as retired individuals, looking for a steady flow of income from their securities. These securities provide cash flow as well as opportunity for some capital appreciation.

LIFE CYCLES AND INVESTMENT STRATEGIES

Investors need to be aware of overriding influences on the company and its industry in order to properly evaluate both the risk and the timing of investment decisions. The price-earnings multiple and future value of shares can be greatly altered by major effects that occur when the perception of a company changes from one investment category to another. The effects of changing interest and inflation rates on investments, overall economic growth, and a myriad of other factors that affect security prices in general need to be understood so that an investment is something more than a gamble. This understanding is best achieved when the information is placed in the perspective of the firm's life cycle.

With this information, overall patterns in the action of stock prices can be discerned. The analysis begins by examining the effects on the price of a company's stock as the company moves through its life cycle. Table 1.3 depicts a sample company, Life-Cycle, Inc. In this and all chapter examples, the concepts behind the numbers, the thought process used to develop them, and the conclusions that can be drawn from them are the focal points.

Table 1.3. Financial history of Life-Cycle, Inc.

Year	Earnings($)	Earnings Growth Rate(%)	P/E Multiple	Stock Price($)	Dividend Yield(%)
1	(.02)	Nil	Nil	3.00	0
2	.15	Nil	30	4.50	0
3	.30	100.0	24	7.20	0
4	.58	93.3	25	14.50	0
5	1.00	72.4	23	23.00	0
6	1.44	44.0	15	21.60	0
7	2.02	40.2	16	32.32	1
8	2.72	34.6	14	38.08	1
9	3.10	13.9	10	31.00	3
10	3.49	12.5	8	27.92	4
11	3.88	11.1	9	34.92	4
12	4.24	9.2	9	38.16	5

On first glance, Life-Cycle, Inc. has had earnings increases each year. However, despite these yearly increases, the growth rate of earnings has declined as the company has matured. Further, as might be expected, the price-earnings multiple of the company has generally declined over the years, while the dividend yield has generally increased.

Given this data, it can be assumed that because the company's earnings increased each year, its stock price should also have increased on a yearly basis. This assumption, predicated on the basis that stock price is fundamentally a function of earnings, seems reasonably sound on the surface. Unfortunately, it lacks the depth of understanding gained by examining a company in relation to its life cycle stage. Remember, throughout the life cycle of a company, investors constantly reevaluate the company's future earnings growth-rate potential. Young, highly concentrated companies typically have the highest future earnings growth-rate potential, whereas older, more diversified companies have lower ones. Additionally, companies with higher growth prospects command higher price-earnings multiples, while companies with lower growth prospects command lower ones. As these companies move through the various stages of their life cycles, their future earnings growth-rate potentials decline, as do the price-earnings multiples that investors are willing to pay for their shares.

Given these facts, Life-Cycle, Inc. would have been considered an aggressive growth stock during years 1 through 5, a growth stock from years 5 through 9, and a mature stock from years 9 through 12. Despite continued earnings advances, the growth rate of earnings was highest during the aggressive growth period, declined as the firm moved into its growth phase, and declined again as the firm moved into its mature phase. By the same token, the price-earnings multiple generally declined throughout the firm's history, with the most dramatic changes occurring during transition from one phase to another. It is interesting to note that the combination of these factors caused price-per-share declines during both transition phases, despite eleven years of uninterrupted earnings growth for the company and considerable earnings growth in the transition years.

This example applies the set of rational analysis techniques described in the company's life cycle stage to the information known about a firm, its industry, and the expectations of investors. In doing this, a reasonable explanation of a commonly seen stock price action has been reached. Specifically, a rational basis for explaining why an individual stock's price can decline despite vibrant earnings growth in the underlying company has been developed. In addition to developing a qualitative thought process that can be used in conjunction with other analytical techniques, this lends a degree of realism to otherwise raw statistical conclusions.

Now examine the effects on the stock prices of several companies within the same industry, given an *expansion* of the overall economic base of that industry. In such a scenario, earnings tend to increase for all firms within the industry in some relation to the earnings that each firm derives from that industry. In examining three exemplary companies—one in the aggressive growth phase of its life cycle (AG, Inc.), the second in the growth phase of its life cycle (GR, Inc.), and the third in the mature phase of its life cycle (MA, Inc.)—reason would dictate that the share price of the aggressive growth firm is likely to appreciate more than either of the others. Why? Consider Table 1.4, constructed from basic information about each company in its particular life cycle stage.

Table 1.4.

Company Name	Current Earnings($)	Earn. from Industry (%)	P/E Multiple	Current Price($)	Dividend Yield (%)	6 Mo. T-bill Rate (%)
AG, Inc.	.50	100	20	10.00	0	6
GR, Inc.	1.00	80	12	12.00	1	6
MA, Inc.	4.00	50	8	32.00	5	6

In this example, AG, GR, and MA generate earnings per share of $0.50, $1, and $4, respectively. Given the phase of each company's life cycle, it is reasonable to presume that 100 percent of AG's, 80 percent of GR's, and only 50 percent of MA's current earnings would be derived from within the industry in question. Furthermore, because investors price each stock in comparison with alternative investments in the same risk category, assigning price-earnings multiples based on some overall market perception of earnings growth and risk, AG would sport the highest, GR the next, and MA the lowest price-earnings multiple. (The example assumes a P/E of 20, 12, and 8, respectively, numbers typical of today's stock market.)

Also based on a firm's stage in its life cycle, MA would have the highest, GR the intermediate, and AG the lowest dividend yield (5 percent, 1 percent, and 0 percent, respectively—again, numbers assumed to be typical of today's stock market).

If overall expansion occurs in the industry, the earnings base of each firm should expand according to the percentage of earnings the company derives from the industry. In this example, let's assume that the industry base and the earnings derived from within the industry double. Table 1.5 illustrates the adjusted earnings level for each firm and the new price of each company's stock, given a constant price-earnings multiple.

Table 1.5.

Company Name	Adjusted Earnings($)	Earn. from Industry (%)	P/E Multiple	Adjusted Price($)	Dividend Yield(%)	6 Mo. T-bill Rate(%)
AG, Inc.	1.00	100	20	20.00	0	6
GR, Inc.	1.80	80	12	21.60	1	6
MA, Inc.	6.00	50	8	48.00	5	6

Using this adjusted information with Table 1.4, it is apparent that the more aggressive the firm and the more concentrated its earnings base is in the expanding industry, the better off the firm will be given such an expansion. Table 1.6 shows the results.

Table 1.6.

Company Name	Current Earnings($)	Current P/E Multiple	Adjusted Earnings($)	Adjusted P/E Multiple	Current Price($)	Adjusted Price($)
AG, Inc.	.50	20	1.00	20	10.00	20.00
GR, Inc.	1.00	12	1.80	12	12.00	21.60
MA, Inc.	4.00	8	6.00	8	32.00	48.00

It is also likely that during an industry expansion such as this, investors may assign higher price-earnings multiples to companies throughout the industry, thereby causing share prices to appreciate that much further. Assuming an across-the-board expansion in these price-earnings multiples of 20 percent, the data can be adjusted as shown in Table 1.7.

Table 1.7.

Company Name	Current Earnings($)	Current P/E Multiple	Adjusted Earnings($)	Adjusted P/E Multiple	Current Price($)	Adjusted Price($)
AG, Inc.	.50	20	1.00	24.0	10.00	24.00
GR, Inc.	1.00	12	1.80	14.4	12.00	25.92
MA, Inc.	4.00	8	6.00	9.6	32.00	57.60

Generalizing the effects of an industry expansion, it is likely that the share prices of all companies within the industry will move higher as a result of improved earnings. Furthermore, stock prices of the most aggressive firms in the industry will appreciate the most while prices for firms in the mature phase will appreciate the least, a typical market phenomena.

Once again, by applying a set of rational techniques to information known regarding the firm, its industry, and the investment expectations of investors, commonly seen stock price action can be explained. In this case, a rational basis has been developed to explain why the price appreciation potential on a percentage basis is higher for more aggressive firms, given an expanding industry. By the same token, reversing the analysis shows why the opposite is also true. By extrapolating the same thought process onto the market in general, investors can see why the whole market moves up when the economy expands, and why more aggressive firms boast higher percentage gains during these upswings.

CONCLUSION

Analyzing various market trends or combinations of trends in conjunction with the application of life cycle analytical techniques leads to understanding the effects various market occurrences might have on an investment portfolio. These techniques bring to light several factors affecting a specific company or industry, factors that might otherwise be overlooked. Specifically, the process developed in this discussion and its corollaries can be summarized as follows:

• All companies, regardless of industry, tend to exemplify the same general characteristics at equivalent stages in their life cycles. From an earnings perspective, what industry a company actually belongs to often is inconsequential.

• Earnings growth rates, including history and future, and investors' changing perception of them, are key determinants in predicting the price-earnings multiples that will be applied to a company's future earnings. Slowing of these growth rates generally foreshadows decline in a company's price-earnings multiple, which in turn leads to a decline in the company's stock price. Thus, it is important to look beyond the level of a company's earnings when attempting to evaluate the underlying value of a stock in relation to its current market price.

• Generally, industry expansion most benefits those firms aggressive in a specific industry, and the stock prices of these companies are likely to boast the highest percentage of appreciation. On the other hand, in an industry contraction, the shares of mature securities are typically affected the least.

• When the economy slows down, mature securities offer better price protection. Conversely, when the economy heats up, industry aggressive companies offer more growth potential. Sophisticated investors lower portfolio risk by selling off aggressive equities in a market upswing, replacing them with mature shares in a market downturn. By doing this, these investors end up being less aggressive at market tops and more aggressive at market bottoms.

• As a general rule, an investment portfolio should not be weighted heavily in any one industry, regardless of category diversification, or in any one category, regardless of industry diversification. A well-balanced investment portfolio provides adequate protection during a market downturn and adequate participation during a market upside.

These generalizations are useful because they represent a rational process through which to focus while conducting fundamental and technical analyses, and should be used in conjunction with these analytical techniques.

2 / FUNDAMENTAL ANALYSIS

OVERVIEW

Fundamental analysis is the process of evaluating a security by analyzing the financial strength of the underlying company. It focuses on *quantitative* factors such as book value, earnings per share, price-earnings ratios, and dividend yield.

Many different fundamental techniques are used to analyze companies, including asset-based, earnings-based, and cash flow-based. Although each may be different in terms of the application of data, all have one thing in common—the source of the data. The primary source for the data used in fundamental analysis is the company's own financial statements—its balance sheet and its net income statement. Audited versions of these statements are furnished to shareholders in the company's annual report; unaudited versions are furnished quarterly. Other good sources for this data include several electronic databases such as CompuServe, Disclosure, and Dow Jones News/Retrieval, and investment publications such as *S&P Stock Reports*, *S&P Industry Reports*, and *Value Line Investment Survey*. Investors may consult these publications to compare the performance of various industries and their leading companies.

Fundamental analysts use this data to run a set of financial calculations that can be evaluated to determine a company's current position. The fundamental analyst compares the company's past and present positions, factors in any new or changing circumstances, and attempts to predict the company's future position. Thus, the company's presumed future position is used to determine the future price of its securities, and a final judgment can be made about the profit potential of these securities.

To analyze a security properly, fundamentalists concentrate on four key areas which they believe affect the price of a security in the open market:

- *Management*—the style, professionalism, and track record of the company's corporate management team.

- *Financial position*—the company's current financial position, as related to the type of business the company is in, the industry in which it operates, the business climate it faces, and the financial position of its competition.
- *Earnings*—the amount of money the company is making and which is ultimately available to shareholders.
- *Market multipliers*—the value placed on the earnings of the company as determined by the price investors are willing to pay to "own" those earnings. These multipliers deal with both company specific and external factors.

Unequivocally, the methodology used to interpolate the data derived from each of these four areas of concentration is different for every fundamental analyst. Therefore, the more information factored into the analysis, the more accurate the analysis becomes.

MANAGEMENT

The analysis of management and management style is not something that someone outside a company can do with relative ease or timeliness, and in a more global sense it may have less value than the effort it cost to acquire the information. That notwithstanding, several avenues are open for investors or potential investors to get some information about management policies and procedures.

A good source for determining management style is an in-depth report on the company written by a Wall Street analyst. Generally, the better-known analysts have developed contacts within the companies they analyze. From these individuals the analysts often get and report information that might shed light on both the company and what the management team is thinking and doing. Detailed reports, such as those prepared for institutional money managers, often include discussions of this nature which can be invaluable sources of information. Nelson Publications produces a guide to such research reports (see Figure 2.1).

Another source for this type of information is the president's letter in the annual report. Typically this letter reveals the type of individual running the company and what he expects of himself, the company, and the people who work in the firm.

Other indicators of management style are insider buying and selling patterns—information which, by law, is publicly available and is followed and reported by several investment publications such as *Barron's*, *Investor's Daily*, and *The Wall Street Journal*.

Figure 2.1. Nelson's listing of Sara Lee

NELSON'S DIRECTORY OF INVESTMENT RESEARCH - 1989

Santa Anita Companies *(cont'd)*

Analyst Coverage:

Audit Investments	
...Kenneth Campbell	201 358-2735
Alex Brown...Robert A. Frank	301 727-1700
Crowell, Weedon...Denny McSweeny	213 620-1850
Lovett Mitchell...Bruce G. Garrison	713 226-5700
Merrill Lynch Research/U.S.	
...Rita Dominguez	212 449-1000
...Jordan Heller	212 449-1000
...Thomas J. Kearns	212 449-1000
PaineWebber...Arthur W. Bullock	212 713-2000

Latest 1988 Research Reports:

Merrill Lynch Research/U.S.	
...Kearns/Dominguez 10/27/88 4pgs	
Crowell, Weedon...Howard 4/1/88 4pgs	
Merrill Lynch Research/U.S.	
...Kearns/Dominguez/Griffin 3/7/88 7pgs	

Santa Fe Energy Partners LP
Houston, TX   SFP/NYSE/12
...   713 783-2401

Prin. Bus.: Oil/Gas Exploration & Productn
Sales (Mil): $131.200
Shareholders: 16,000
Shares Outs.: 32,176,000
Market Val (Mil): $498.728

Pres:	J.L. Payne
CFO:	L.J. Billes
Treas:	H.J. Farley
Cont:	M.S. Wilkes
IRC:	P.W. Bode
Sec:	D.A. Louden
GC:	D.L. Hicks

Analyst Coverage:

Gruntal & Co....Joseph Battipaglia	212 858-6000
Robert A. Stanger Co.	
...Nancy T. Schabel	201 389-3600
Tucker, Anthony...Everett G. Titus, III	212 618-7400

Santa Fe Southern Pacific Corp
Chicago, IL   SFX/NYSE/12   312 786-6422
Prin. Bus.: Railroads/Real Estate
Other Bus.: Real Estate
Sales (Mil): $5,448.400
Employees: 48,700
Shareholders: 90,000
Shares Outs.: 157,106,000
Market Val (Mil): $3,083.990
Institutions Own: 40%
Pension Fund Assets (Mil): $930

Chmn:	Robert D. Krebs 47 (23 yrs)
CEO:	Robert D. Krebs
Pres:	Robert D. Krebs
CFO:	Orval M. Adam
Treas:	Orval M. Adam
IRC:	William F. Todd
CC:	Robert E. Gehrt
Sec:	J. F. Donohoe
GC:	J. F. Donohoe
PFO:	David J. Meagher 43 (6 yrs)
EB:	Russ E. Hagberg
P&D:	Fred D. Watson
RE:	O. G. Linde
CM:	Marsha K. Morgan
RM:	J. A. Cornelius
MIS:	John W. Curtis

Analyst Coverage:

Argus Research...Mark F. Degenhart	212 425-7500
Audit Investments	
...Kenneth Campbell	201 358-2735
Bear Stearns...Gary Schneider	212 272-2000
Alex Brown...Sally H. Smith	301 727-1700
Brown Brothers Harriman	
...Kathleen A. Lally	212 483-1818
Dillon, Read...Susan Chapman	212 906-7000
Donaldson Lufkin & Jenrette	
...Joel Price (*3)	212 504-3000
...Luella White Price	212 504-3000
Drexel Burnham Lambert	
...Linda Dunn	212 232-5000

Santa Fe Southern Pacific Corp *(cont'd)*

First Boston	
...Graeme Anne Lidgerwood (*R)	212 909-2000
Fitch Investors...John W. Walsh (B)	212 668-8300
Goldman, Sachs	
...Michael R. Armellino (*1)	212 902-1000
Gruntal & Co.	
...George O. Zimmermann	212 858-6000
Kidder, Peabody...D. Christine King	212 510-3000
Moody's Investors Service	
...Robert Ray (B)	212 553-0300
Morgan Stanley	
...Andras R. Petery (*3)	212 703-4000
Louis Nicoud & Associates	
...F. Barry Nelson	212 233-3465
E Magnus Oppenheim	
...E. Magnus Oppenheim	212 421-1818
...Jonathan Schwartz	212 421-1818
Oppenheimer...O. Lee Tawes, III	212 667-7000
...Gary Yablon	212 667-7000
PaineWebber...Anthony B. Hatch	212 713-2000
...James M. Voytko (*2)	212 713-2000
Pershing & Co....Joan T. Goodman	312-294-0591
Prescott Ball & Turben	
...George G. Morris	216 574-7300
Printon, Kane...Isabel H. Benham	212 355-0155
Provident National Bank	
...Andrew Geller	215 585-5000
Shearson Lehman Hutton	
...Burton M. Strauss, Jr. (*R)	212 298-2000
Wertheim Schroder	
...Jeffrey B. Stone (*R)	212 492-6000

Latest 1988 Research Reports:

Dillon, Read...Chapman 10/25/88 4pgs	
Dillon, Read...Chapman 8/11/88 6pgs	
Oppenheimer...Yablon 6/26/88 2pgs	
Louis Nicoud & Associates...Nelson 5/23/88 2pgs	
Donaldson Lufkin & Jenrette	
...Price (*)/Price 5/16/88	

Sara Lee Corporation
Chicago, IL   SLE/NYSE/06   312 726-2600
Prin. Bus.: Food & non-food consumer prod.
Sales (Mil): $9,155.000
Employees: 92,400
Shareholders: 50,000
Shares Outs.: 110,724,000
Market Val (Mil): $4,775.526
Institutions Own: 39%
Pension Fund Assets (Mil): $576

Chmn:	John H. Bryan, Jr. 53 (31 yrs)
CEO:	John H. Bryan, Jr.
Pres:	John B. McKinnon
CFO:	Michael E. Murphy 53 (10 yrs)
Treas:	Mary Ellen Johnson 42 (3 yrs)
Cont:	Daniel R. Kulik
IRC:	Andrea Stack
CC:	Anne McCarthy
Sec:	Gordon H. Newman
GC:	Gordon H. Newman
PFO:	James C. Clousing
EB:	James C. Clousing
P&D:	C. Steven McMillan
RE:	Thomas Gordon
Lsg:	Raymond C. Howick
CM:	Mary Ellen Johnson
RM:	William D. Irle
MIS:	Vincent H. Swoyer

Analyst Coverage:

Argus Research	
...Pavlos M. Alexandrakis	212 425-7500
Bear Stearns...June D. Page	212 272-2000
William Blair...Thomas R. Kully	312 236-1600
Blunt Ellis...Richard G. Elam	414 347-3400
Brown Brothers Harriman	
...William J. Wason	212 483-1818
County NatWest USA	
...Timothy S. Ramey	212 440-8440
Dain Bosworth...L. Craig Carver	612 371-2711
Deutsche Bank Capital Corp	
...David M. Hill	212 612-0600

Sara Lee Corporation *(cont'd)*

Donaldson Lufkin & Jenrette	
...William Leach	212 504-3000
Drexel Burnham Lambert	
...Joanna Scharf	212 232-5000
A. G. Edwards...John C. Bierbusse	314 289-3000
Fahnestock & Co....David Goldman	212 668-8000
First Boston...Eric Larson	212 909-2000
First Manhattan...Beth Loewy	212 832-4400
Fourteen Research...Sally L. Schaadt	212 286-0800
Goldman, Sachs...Nomi Ghez	212 902-1000
Gruntal & Co....Mun Yee Chan	212 858-6000
Janney Montgomery	
...Marvin B. Roffman	215 665-6000
Edward D. Jones...Bob Bernstein	314 851-2000
Josephthal...Janet Mangano	212 577-3000
Kirkpatrick, Pettis...Marcia A. Koory	402 449-1400
Legg Mason Wood Walker	
...R. Hutchings Vernon	301 539-3400
McKinley Allsopp...George V. Novello	212 980-5300
Merrill Lynch Research/U.S.	
...William Maguire	212 449-1000
Moran & Associates, Inc.	
...Frederick A. Moran	203 661-9600
Oppenheimer...O. Lee Tawes, III	212 667-7000
PaineWebber...Roger W. Spencer	312 580-8000
Pershing & Co....Edward Froelich	212 312-2000
Piper Jaffray...Stephen M. Carnes	612 342-6000
Prudential Bache...John M. McMillin	212 214-1023
Salomon Bros...Bonnie M. Rivers	404 827-7740
Smith Barney...Ronald B. Morrow	212 698-6000
Swiss Bank Corporation Investment	
banking...Michael J. Warshawsky	212 938-7400
S.G. Warburg & Co.	
...Harry A. Ikenson	212 459-7000

Latest 1988 Research Reports:

Bear Stearns...Page 11/4/88 4pgs	
County NatWest USA...Ramey 11/2/88 6pgs	
Merrill Lynch Research/U.S.	
...Maguire (*) 11/1/88 4pgs	
Goldman, Sachs...Ghez (*) 10/31/88 12pgs	
William Blair...Kully 10/25/88 10pgs	

Satellite Music Network Inc.
Dallas, TX   SMNI/NASD/12   214 991-9200
Prin. Bus.: Broadcasting
Sales (Mil): $15.786
Employees: 130
Shareholders: 2,000
Shares Outs.: 8,964,000
Market Val (Mil): $37.021
Institutions Own: 4%

Chmn:	John S. Tyler
CEO:	John S. Tyler
Pres:	John S. Tyler
CFO:	David N. Hubschman
Treas:	David N. Hubschman
IRC:	Marianne Bellinger
Sec:	David N. Hubschman

Analyst Coverage:

CL Global Partners...Jessica Reif	212 428-6100
Kidder, Peabody...Andrew W. Marcus	212 510-3000
Wertheim Schroder	
...Francine S. Blum	212 492-6000
...David J. Londoner	212 492-6000

Latest 1988 Research Reports:

Wertheim Schroder	
...Blum/Londoner (*) 1/25/88 9pgs	

Savannah Foods & Ind Inc
Savannah, GA   SVAN/NASD/12
...   912 234-1261
Prin. Bus.: Sugar
Sales (Mil): $591.340
Employees: 1,266
Shareholders: 2,657
Shares Outs.: 6,675,000
Market Val (Mil): $220.275
Institutions Own: 18%
Pension Fund Assets (Mil): $43

CEO:	William W. Sprague, Jr.
Pres:	William W. Sprague, Jr.

Source: Reprinted from *Nelson's Directory of Investment Research*, 1989. © 1989 Nelson Publications, P.O. Box 591, Port Chester, NY 10573.

FINANCIAL POSITION

The two primary financial statements issued by a company are the income statement and the balance sheet. They are distinctly different in their creation and purpose, and each tells an entirely different story about the company. A third statement, the cash flow statement, combines data from the income statement and the balance sheet.

The balance sheet, a company's statement of assets, liabilities, and shareholders' equity, provides a picture of the company's financial position; it is designed to state the position of a company at a specific moment in time. Typically the balance sheet is calculated and reported on both a quarterly and an annual basis.

A company's assets must be exactly equal to the sum of its liabilities and shareholders' equity—that is, in balance. The balance sheet shows that every dollar invested in assets owned by the com-

Figure 2.2. Balance sheet of Sara Lee Corporation

CONSOLIDATED BALANCE SHEETS

(in thousands except share data)	July 2, 1988	June 27, 1987	June 28, 1986
Current assets			
Cash and equivalents	$ 178,552	$ 302,862	$ 156,159
Trade accounts receivable, less allowances of			
$54,850 in 1988, $47,084 in 1987 and $43,672			
in 1986	717,532	609,998	650,986
Inventories			
Finished goods	674,186	640,723	579,107
Work in process	109,213	86,382	72,466
Materials and supplies	344,054	284,614	284,753
	1,127,453	1,011,719	936,326
Other current assets	65,335	35,827	36,010
Total current assets	2,088,872	1,960,406	1,779,481
Investments in unconsolidated companies	88,763	116,320	43,366
Trademarks and other assets	258,053	230,133	184,965
Property, at cost			
Land	64,203	51,023	46,670
Buildings and improvements	822,594	720,741	577,046
Machinery and equipment	1,345,120	1,356,151	1,095,171
Construction in progress	210,043	100,354	58,865
Assets under capital leases	42,599	38,700	40,265
	2,484,559	2,266,969	1,818,017
Accumulated depreciation	1,067,855	1,026,399	821,756
Property, net	1,416,704	1,240,570	996,261
Intangible assets	1,159,678	644,246	499,033
	$5,012,070	$4,191,675	$3,503,106

The accompanying Notes to Financial Statements are an integral part of these balance sheets.

pany originated from either a liability incurred by the company or, in one form or another, from the shareholders. In essence, then, the balance sheet represents a list of all assets balanced against a list of all liabilities and shareholder claims.

In an effort to accumulate the many individual asset, liability, and shareholder equity items held by a company, the balance sheet combines similar assets into categories and reports only category totals rather than individual items. Figure 2.2 is a balance sheet of the Sara Lee Corporation, which manufactures, markets, and distributes food and consumer packaged goods through retail and food service outlets as well as through direct mail. Sara Lee will be used throughout this book to help illustrate how to apply the investment topics as they are presented.

Though the following definitions are not complete accounting definitions for balance sheet terms, they do represent good working definitions for concepts discussed in this chapter (for additional

Figure 2.2. Balance sheet of Sara Lee Corporation, *Continued*

Sara Lee Corporation and Subsidiaries

	July 2, 1988	June 27, 1987	June 28, 1986
Current liabilities			
Notes payable	$ 94,599	$ 219,354	$ 95,611
Accounts payable	769,733	510,580	404,605
Accrued liabilities	905,180	766,322	595,604
Accrued income taxes	11,813	20,892	39,745
Current maturities of long-term debt	22,145	75,993	13,485
Current obligations under capital leases	2,691	2,121	2,017
Total current liabilities	1,806,161	1,595,262	1,151,067
Long-term debt	877,014	617,424	617,267
Long-term obligations under capital leases	16,420	15,200	16,895
Deferred income taxes	298,952	280,527	282,705
Other liabilities	213,426	192,307	205,494
Convertible adjustable preferred stock: 1,500,000 shares issued and outstanding, redeemable at $50 per share	75,000	75,000	75,000
Auction preferred stock: 1,500 shares issued and outstanding, redeemable at $100,000 per share	150,000	—	—
Common stockholders' equity			
Common stock: 119,596,068 shares issued in 1988 and 1987, and 59,798,034 in 1986	159,461	159,461	79,730
Capital surplus	24,212	3,667	6,965
Retained earnings	1,597,259	1,408,504	1,320,475
Foreign currency translation	15,337	20,048	(42,350)
Treasury stock, at cost: 9,037,505 shares in 1988, 8,872,115 shares in 1987 and 6,416,223 in 1986	(221,172)	(175,725)	(210,142)
Total common stockholders' equity	1,575,097	1,415,955	1,154,678
	$5,012,070	$4,191,675	$3,503,106

Source: Sara Lee Corporation, 1988 Annual Report

terms used throughout this book, refer to the Glossary):

- *Common stock*—stock with no preferential claims on income and assets, sometimes referred to as the claims held by the "true" owners of the company.
- *Current*—items that will be affected in the present, or current, year. Asset-based items include cash, accounts receivable, and inventory. Liabilities include notes payable, accounts payable, accrued liabilities, and accrued income taxes. Portions of the long-term debt or obligations under capital leases that are due within the current year also are included under the "current" section of the balance sheet.
- *Fixed*—those items that will not be affected in the current year, such as property, trademarks, and intangible assets. Sara Lee does not apply the term fixed to its balance sheet, but the figure is composed of the items below the total current asset figure on the asset side of the balance sheet, less the accumulated depreciation.
- *Foreign currency translation*—gains or losses from foreign currency-denominated assets and liabilities, incurred because of currency fluctuation.
- *Intangible*—items with a value difficult to determine, such as trademarks and goodwill. Sara Lee breaks out "trademarks" from the overall "intangible" category.
- *Long term*—liability items that will not be affected in the current year, such as debt not due within the year, capital leases and deferred income taxes.
- *Miscellaneous, sundry,* or *other*—physical items that are being held for an indefinite period of time and thus are not involved in the company's day-to-day business (such as unimproved land).
- *Paid-in capital* (or *Capital surplus*)—the difference between the price actually received by the company for the common stock and its par value, if any.
- *Preferred stock*—the par value of stock having preferential claim on income and assets.
- *Retained earnings* (or *Earned surplus*)—undistributed corporate profits.
- *Treasury stock*—common stock that the company has repurchased.

From the balance sheet alone, a variety of measures can be calculated to determine and evaluate a company's position. These include:

- *Capital structure*—the capital makeup of the company, as determined by how much of the assets are paid for by the debt, preferred stock, or equity.
- *Collateral*—the relative worth behind the company's outstanding securities, as determined by the book value, net assets per bond, and net assets per preferred share ratios.
- *Leverage*—the amount of nonequity capital the company is using in its capital structure (see debt-to-asset and debt-to-equity ratios later in this chapter).
- *Liquidity*—the company's ability to raise cash (see cash, current, and quick asset ratios).

EARNINGS

A company's earnings are calculated and presented in the income statement, also called the earnings statement or statement of operations. The *income statement* reviews the activities of a company over a specific period of time. It, too, is calculated and reported on both a quarterly and an annual basis. The income statement reports three things: how much income has been earned for the period, how much expense has been incurred to earn the income, and how much profit or net income, if any, is left over.

As related to the balance sheet, the income statement provides a breakdown of what changes occurred to retained earnings during the period. So, if balance sheets were created immediately before and after the period in question, the income statement would show how the change in retained earnings came about. Also, as with the balance sheet, the income statement agglomerates the myriad transactions that occurred during the period into a few categories, reporting only the category totals. Most statements include categories similar to those of Sara Lee, in Figure 2.3.

The following represents working definitions, to assist in studying Figure 2.3 (for complete accounting definitions and terminology, refer to the Glossary):

- *Cost of sales* (or *Cost of goods sold*)—the costs incurred in making the products that were sold.
- *Depreciation*—the expenses attributed to the use of the company's fixed assets as apportioned over the accounting life of those assets. Sara Lee did not categorize this accounting expense in the income statement; however, some companies will. Sara Lee did include the figure in its cash flow statement.

Figure 2.3. Income Statement of Sara Lee Corporation

CONSOLIDATED STATEMENTS OF INCOME   Sara Lee Corporation and Subsidiaries

(in thousands except per share data)	July 2, 1988	June 27, 1987	June 28, 1986
Net sales	**$10,423,816**	$9,154,588	$7,937,722
Cost of sales	7,096,756	6,309,565	5,403,149
Selling, general and administrative expenses	2,717,504	2,328,704	2,122,809
Interest expense	119,925	105,632	73,110
Interest income	(23,705)	(37,159)	(16,943
	9,910,480	8,706,742	7,582,125
Income before income taxes	513,336	447,846	355,597
Income taxes	188,261	180,787	132,142
Net income	**325,075**	267,059	223,455
Preferred dividend requirements	(9,394)	(4,125)	(4,491
Earnings available for common stockholders	$ 315,681	$ 262,934	$ 218,964
Net income per common share	**$2.83**	$2.35	$2.02
Average shares outstanding	111,670	111,687	108,211

The accompanying Notes to Financial Statements are an integral part of these statements.

Source: Sara Lee Corporation, 1988 Annual Report

- *Earnings available for common stockholders*—the income that common stockholders are entitled to after debtholders and preferred stockholders have been paid.
- *Earnings before interest and taxes (EBIT)*—the net income for the period after all expenses have been paid except for interest and taxes. Sara Lee did not include this category in its income statement, but it can be computed by adding interest expense to income before taxes and subtracting interest income.
- *Earnings before taxes (EBT, or income before taxes)*—the net income for the period after all expenses have been paid, except for taxes.
- *General and administrative expenses*—all direct costs incurred in generating revenue, such as wages. Some firms will also group cost of goods sold to this category.
- *Gross sales*—the total operating revenue for the period, irrespective of the product or service the company may be selling. Sara Lee did not report on gross sales in its income statement, but other companies do. If reported, it would precede "net sales" and "returns."

- *Interest*—all charges that must be paid on the company's liabilities.
- *Net income*—the net earnings of the company for the period after all expenses have been paid.
- *Net income per common share*—earnings available for common stockholders divided by the shares outstanding.
- *Net sales*—the net operating revenue for the period, after returns have been paid back.
- *Operating income*—the net operating income for the period, after all expenses have been paid except for interest and taxes. Sara Lee did not differentiate this category; however, by subtracting cost of sales and selling, general, and administrative expenses from net sales, operating income can be computed.
- *Other income*—other net income earned by the company from all sources other than normal operations, such as investment income. Sara Lee refers to this category as "interest income."
- *Preferred dividend requirements*—the dividends that are paid to preferred stockholders.
- *Returns*—the gross dollars of refunds given for sales that were returned or refused. Returns were not reported in Sara Lee's income statement.
- *Taxes*—the government's charges that are paid on the company's net earnings.

From the income statement alone, a company's coverage can be calculated. *Coverage* is the extent to which the company's earnings cover its anticipated cash outlays, as determined by the fixed charges, interest, preferred dividend coverages, as well as the payout ratio.

Using company data from both the balance sheet and the income statement, a number of additional measures can be calculated:

- *Activity*—the amount of revenue the company is generating as related to the amount of assets it has deployed. (See the average collection period, fixed asset turnover, inventory turnover, receivables turnover, and total asset turnover ratios later in this chapter.)
- *Earnings*—the amount of profit generated by the company that is ultimately available to shareholders. (Earnings ratios include earnings per share, fully diluted earnings per share, and primary earnings per share.)
- *Profitability*—the amount of profit generated by the company relative to its activity and assets deployed. (See operating, profit

margin, return on assets, return on equity, and return on invested capital ratios.)

These measures are then compared against other measures and against those of other companies, as previously discussed.

Sometimes in the normal course of business, extraordinary events occur that may have dramatic effects on the income statement for the period. For example, suppose a company bought a piece of property in downtown Manhattan during the early part of the twentieth century with the intention to eventually build its headquarters there. Then, after eighty years of holding the property, the company decides to sell. The gain on this asset, which is sure to be significant and is unequivocally an extraordinary event, could have a dramatic effect on the income statement if it were simply included as "other income." In order to avoid confusion, such transactions are segregated and treated as "extraordinary" or "nonrecurring" items and reported in the notes to financial statements.

Myriad circumstances can result in an extraordinary gain or loss for a company. Some of the more typical transactions that are classified as extraordinary, and therefore segregated, include:

- any material gains or losses on the sale of assets,
- the write-down or write-off of goodwill,
- the condemnation or expropriation of assets,
- any major changes in the valuation of foreign currencies, and
- the sale of any significant portion of the business.

Statement of Cash Flows

The statement of cash flows provides a summary of the company's cash transactions over a period of time. It lists inflows and outflows of cash, much like a checkbook. Figure 2.4 shows Sara Lee's cash flow statement. The statement, found in the annual report, is broken down into operating, investing, and financing activities. This allows investors to see where the money was flowing from as well as where it was being used.

When computing income, depreciation is subtracted from sales (see income statement). However, depreciation is really an accounting concept; it does not reflect the flow of money, so to determine cash flow it should be added back into net income. For example, in 1988 Sara Lee had a total cash flow from operating activities of $732,280,000 (in all of the statements, Sara Lee has presented the figures in thousands):

Figure 2.4. Cash flow statement of Sara Lee Corporation

CONSOLIDATED STATEMENTS OF CASH FLOWS   Sara Lee Corporation and Subsidiaries

		Year Ended	
(in thousands)	July 2, 1988	June 27, 1987	June 28, 1986
CASH FLOWS FROM OPERATING ACTIVITIES			
Net income	$ 325,075	$ 267,059	$ 223,455
Adjustments for non-cash items included in net income:			
Depreciation and amortization	197,838	168,027	141,723
Increase (decrease) in deferred income taxes	15,102	(10,629)	(19,305)
Other non-cash charges	42,185	4,635	56,652
Change in current assets and liabilities	152,080	227,536	(154,895)
Net cash flows from operating activities	732,280	656,628	247,630
CASH FLOWS FROM INVESTING ACTIVITIES			
Purchases of property and equipment	(448,974)	(286,547)	(221,725)
Acquisitions of businesses	(890,653)	(236,293)	(57,669)
Investments in unconsolidated companies	3,192	(86,216)	(7,151)
Sales of businesses	227,243	70,870	138,235
Sales of property	157,235	32,237	13,479
Other	10,665	2,211	6,736
Net cash flows from investing activities	(941,292)	(503,738)	(128,095)
CASH FLOWS FROM FINANCING ACTIVITIES			
Issuance of auction preferred stock	150,000	—	—
Issuances of common stock	34,028	49,526	22,164
Purchases of treasury stock	(91,653)	(100,003)	(70,370)
Borrowings of long-term debt	393,092	10,916	156,448
Repayments of long-term debt	(122,994)	(37,624)	(40,586)
Short-term borrowings (repayments), net	(124,755)	123,743	(68,268)
Payments of dividends	(136,320)	(106,273)	(87,870)
Other	(2,866)	(3,892)	(5,799)
Net cash flows from financing activities	98,532	(63,607)	(94,281)
Effect of exchange rate changes on cash	(13,830)	57,420	26,759
Increase (decrease) in cash and equivalents	(124,310)	146,703	52,013
Cash and equivalents at beginning of year	302,862	156,159	104,146
Cash and equivalents at end of year	$ 178,552	$ 302,862	$ 156,159
THE COMPONENTS OF THE CHANGE IN CURRENT ASSETS AND LIABILITIES FOLLOW:			
(Increase) decrease in trade accounts receivable	$ 49,199	$ 104,865	$ (73,279)
(Increase) in inventories	(38,207)	(31,556)	(115,987)
(Increase) decrease in other current assets	(25,127)	2,961	(2,930)
Increase (decrease) in accounts payable	109,482	67,570	(14,213)
Increase in accrued liabilities	91,996	111,063	33,398
Increase (decrease) in accrued income taxes	(35,263)	(27,367)	18,116
Change in current assets and liabilities	$ 152,080	$ 227,536	$(154,895)
Supplemental disclosures of cash flow information:			
Cash paid during the year for:			
Interest	$ 110,474	$ 94,286	$ 66,912
Income taxes	215,661	222,048	133,884

SFAS 95, "Statement of Cash Flows," was adopted in 1988 and prior years were restated to be consistent with the current year's presentation.
The accompanying Notes to Financial Statements are an integral part of these statements.

Source: Sara Lee Corporation, 1988 Annual Report

Net income	$325,075,000
Depreciation/amortization	197,838,000
Increase (decrease) deferred income taxes	15,102,000
Other non-cash charges	42,185,000
Change in current assets/liabilities	152,080,000
Cash Flow from Operating Activities	**$732,280,000**

The cash flow from investing activities tracks how cash was spent on the purchase of new plant and equipment, the acquisitions of new and consolidated companies, and the sales of businesses and properties. From this report we can see that Sara Lee spent much more on new property, equipment, and acquisitions than it divested. A net amount of $941,292,000 of cash was *spent* for future growth of Sara Lee:

Purchase of property & equipment	$(448,974,000)
Acquisitions of businesses	(890,653,000)
Investments in unconsolidated companies	3,192,000
Sales of businesses	227,243,000
Sales of property	157,235,000
Other	10,665,000
Cash Flow from Investing Activities	**$(941,292,000)**

Cash flow from financing activities reports on whether the company is receiving money from issuing debt or equity, or spending cash to reduce debt or equity. This report shows that Sara Lee had an inflow of cash amounting to $98,532,000 from its financing activities:

Issuance of auction preferred stock	$150,000,000
Issuances of common stock	34,028,000
Purchases of treasury stock	(91,653,000)
Borrowings of long-term debt	393,092,000
Repayments of long-term debt	(122,994,000)
Short-term borrowings (repayments), net	(124,755,000)
Payments of dividends	(136,320,000)
Other	(2,866,000)
Cash Flow from Financing Activities	**$98,532,000**

Sara Lee holds assets in foreign-denominated currencies, so the exchange gains or losses have been added or subtracted to or from the cash amount. The overall increase or decrease for cash from operating activities, investing activities, financing, and exchange rate effects is determined for the year and added to the beginning cash balance to determine the amount of cash at year end. Sara Lee had a decrease of $124,310,000 in cash during 1988, so that its cash position decreased from $302,862,000 to $178,552,000:

Cash flow-Operating activities	$732,280,000
Cash flow-Investing activities	(941,292,000)
Cash flow-Financing activities	98,532,000
Effect of exchange rate charges on cash	(13,830,000)
1988 Increase (decrease) in cash equivalents	($124,310,000)
1987 Cash and Equivalents (end of year)	$302,862,000
1988 Increase (decrease) in cash equivalents	($124,310,000)
1988 Cash and Equivalents (end of year)	*$178,552,000*

The bottom portion of the statement of cash flows examines the increase (or decrease) in other current assets and liabilities.

The statement of cash flows helps determine whether money came in from operating, investing, or financing activities, and it helps determine why a company's amount of cash is increasing or decreasing.

The following section provides specific formulas to assist investors in examining a company's financial statements. Each formula is followed with an example using Sara Lee Corporation. Remember, each ratio should be examined in the context of the company's other ratios, in comparison to other companies within the same industry, and in comparison to itself over time.

FUNDAMENTAL ANALYSIS: FINANCIAL STATEMENT RATIOS

ACTIVITY MEASURES

Activity measures test the efficiency of the company's use of its assets.

AVERAGE COLLECTION PERIOD

Data Sources: Balance Sheet and Income Statement

$$\text{Average Collection Period} = \frac{\text{Net accounts receivable} \times 365 \text{ days}}{\text{Net sales}}$$

Where:
▸ *net accounts receivable* means money due from customers within the current year, less any provisions for returns, trade discounts for early payments, and bad debts.
▸ *net sales* means gross sales, less any discounts, returns, and refunds.

Measure:
Average collection period is a measure of the speed at which the company turns sales into cash.

Interpretation:
A low average collection period can signal highly efficient collections and efficient asset utilization. If it is too low, it can warn that the company has a very stringent collection policy and may be losing potential sales.

A high average collection period can signal poor sales, slow collections, or a very lenient collection policy in which sales are being made but not paid for. By comparing the average collection period to the stated collection policy found within the company's annual report, a judgment can be made as to which problem exists.

An increasing average collection period can signal either slowing sales or slowing payments, both of which foretell potential problems for the company. A declining average collection period can signal increasing sales, more efficient asset utilization, or tighter management controls.

Example: Average Collection Period

$$1988 = \frac{717,532 \text{ X } 365}{10,423,816} = 25.13 \text{ days} \qquad\qquad 1987 = 24.32 \text{ days}$$

Sara Lee's average collection period increased from 24.32 days in 1987 to 25.13 days in 1988. This means that in 1988, approximately 25 days passed between the time a customer was billed and when the invoice was paid. A one-day increase in the average collection period is minor, and Sara Lee's average collection period is common for companies in the food industry, which averages 26 days.

FIXED ASSET TURNOVER

Data Sources: Balance Sheet and Income Statement

$$\text{Fixed Asset Turnover} = \frac{\text{Net sales}}{\text{Fixed assets}}$$

Where:
▸ *net sales* means gross sales, less any discounts, returns, and refunds.
▸ *fixed assets* means physical assets such as property, plant, and equipment used by the company in its current operations, which are not expected to be converted into cash within the current year.

Measure:
Fixed asset turnover is a measure of the speed with which a company turns over the money it has invested in fixed assets.

Interpretation:
Generally, the higher the fixed asset turnover ratio, the more efficiently the company is operating. An investor should compare the company to its industry to help determine whether the level is relatively high or low.

A high fixed asset turnover ratio can indicate highly efficient production procedures, or it can indicate inadequate investment in fixed assets. The former situation can be exceptionally advantageous for the company; the latter can stifle the company's long-term prospects.

A low fixed asset turnover ratio can signal poor sales relative to the amount of money invested in property, plant, and equipment, and can be due to a number of things, including inefficient production procedures, poor production controls, or bad purchase decisions.

A declining ratio can signal anything from slowing sales, declining efficiency, and aging equipment, to the company becoming more capital intensive in its production procedures. An increasing ratio can signal increasing sales, improved efficiency, or better asset utilization.

Example: Fixed Asset Turnover

$$1988 = \frac{10,423,816}{1,416,704} = 7.36 \qquad\qquad 1987 = 7.38$$

Sara Lee's fixed asset turnover did not change in 1988. An increase in fixed assets has kept up with the increase in sales. Sara Lee's fixed asset turnover is slightly higher than the industry average of about 7, indicating an efficient operation.

INVENTORY TURNOVER

Data Sources: Balance Sheet and Income Statement

Two commonly used methods:

$$\text{Inventory Turnover} = \frac{\text{Net sales}}{\text{Year-end inventory}} \quad *$$

or

$$\text{Inventory Turnover} = \frac{\text{Cost of goods sold}}{\text{Year-end inventory}}$$

Where:
> ▸ *net sales* means gross sales, less any discounts, returns, and refunds.
> ▸ *year-end inventory* means raw materials, work in progress, and finished merchandise waiting for sale, valued at the lower of cost or market value.
> ▸ *cost of goods sold* means the cost of the inventory sold during the period.

Measure:
Inventory turnover ratio is a measure of the speed at which the company sells its inventory.

Interpretation:
Generally, the higher the inventory turnover ratio, the more efficiently the company is operating. A high inventory turnover ratio can signal anything from highly efficient inventory control procedures to insufficient inventory levels. A high inventory turnover ratio is generally good, but if it is caused by insufficient inventory levels, it may result in lost sales or back orders.

A low inventory turnover ratio can signal poor sales or high inventory levels. A low inventory turnover ratio indicates that too much money is tied up in inventory relative to the sales level of the company, and the costs associated with carrying that inventory are high.

A declining ratio can signal slowing sales, bulging inventories, or inefficient use of the company's assets. An increasing ratio can signal a pickup in sales or tighter management controls.

Example: Inventory Turnover

$$1988 = \frac{10{,}423{,}816}{1{,}127{,}453} = 9.25 \qquad\qquad 1987 = 9.05$$

or

$$1988 = \frac{7{,}096{,}756}{1{,}127{,}453} = 6.29 \qquad\qquad 1987 = 6.24$$

Sara Lee has made slight improvements in its inventory turnover, indicating a slightly more efficient inventory control.

---

* Dividing sales by year-end inventory is the more common method of determining inventory turnover. The second method is a good way to determine if changes in the turnover ratio are due to better inventory management or changes in the profit margins. The large difference between the two ratios occurs since one measures inventory against sales, and the other measures inventory against the cost of the goods.

RECEIVABLES TURNOVER

Data Sources: Balance Sheet and Income Statement

$$\text{Receivables Turnover} = \frac{\text{Net sales}}{\text{Net accounts receivable}}$$

Where:

▶ *net sales* means gross sales, less any discounts, returns, and refunds.

▶ *net accounts receivable* means money due from customers within the current year, less any provisions for returns, trade discounts for early payments, and bad debts.

Measure:

Receivables turnover ratio is a measure of the speed at which the company turns sales into cash.

Interpretation:

Generally, the higher the receivables turnover ratio, the more efficiently the company is operating. A high receivables turnover ratio can signal highly efficient collections and efficient asset utilization. It can also mean that the company has a too-stringent collection policy and therefore may be losing potential sales.

A low receivables turnover ratio can signal poor sales or slow collections, or it can indicate that the collection policy of the company is too lenient and that sales are not being paid for.

A declining ratio can signal slowing sales or slowing payments —both potential problems for the company. An increasing ratio may signal higher sales levels, more efficient asset utilization, or tighter management controls.

This ratio is inversely proportional to the average collection period. If there is a decline in the average collection period, the receivables turnover will increase.

Example: Receivables Turnover

$$1988 = \frac{10,423,816}{717,532} = 14.53 \qquad\qquad 1987 = 15.01$$

Sara Lee has experienced a slight decline in its receivables turnover ratio. This is no surprise because of the increase in the average collection period. Sales increased over 13% in 1988, so the decline is not due to slower sales levels. Also, sales allowances have kept pace with sales, so there are no collection policy problems. The receivables turnover *did* decline over the period because receivables grew slightly faster than sales. As slight as this change is, investors need not worry.

TOTAL ASSET TURNOVER

Data Sources: Balance Sheet and Income Statement

$$\text{Total Asset Turnover} = \frac{\text{Net sales}}{\text{Total assets}}$$

Where:
  ▸ *net sales* means gross sales, less any discounts, returns, and refunds.
  ▸ *total assets* means all assets owned by the company—whether they are currently being used or not—including current, fixed, sundry, and intangible assets.

Measure:
Total asset turnover is a measure of the revenue generated by the company's invested assets.

Interpretation:
Generally, the higher the total asset turnover ratio, that is the more sales per dollar of invested capital, the more efficiently the company is operating. However, an unreasonably high total asset turnover ratio can signal that the company lacks sufficient infrastructure or is in need of more capital with which to operate. Reading the annual report and analyst reviews could help determine how to properly interpret total asset turnover.

A low total asset turnover ratio can signal poor sales or general inefficiency. It can also signal that the company has assets deployed in an inefficient fashion—that is, the company is not generating sufficient sales to justify the assets it has deployed.

A declining ratio can signal anything from slowing sales, declining efficiency, and aging equipment, to a company generating excess cash that is being poorly used. An increasing ratio usually means increasing sales and better asset utilization.

Example: Total Asset Turnover

$$1988 = \frac{10,423,816}{5,012,070} = 2.08 \qquad\qquad\qquad 1987 = 2.18$$

Total asset turnover decreased slightly for Sara Lee even though sales increased over 13% in 1988. An examination of the balance sheet reveals that there was a great increase in intangible assets. Intangible assets are those assets in which actual value is difficult or impossible to determine, such as goodwill, copyrights, patents, trademarks, or leasehold improvements. In 1988, Sara Lee acquired Akzo Consumenten Produkten and several other smaller firms, which increased its intangible asset base.

COLLATERAL MEASURES

Collateral measures attempt to determine how many dollars of real tangible assets stand behind various classes of securities. They are helpful in identifying those securities that may be improperly covered in the event the company were to go under.

BOOK VALUE PER SHARE OF COMMON STOCK

Data Source: Balance Sheet

$$\text{Book Value} = \frac{\text{Common stock - Intangibles}}{\text{Number of shares of common stock outstanding}}*$$

or

$$\text{Book Value} = \frac{\text{Common stock}}{\text{Number of shares of common stock outstanding}}**$$

Where:

▶ *common stock* means all stock that has no preferential claims to income or assets.

▶ *intangibles* means all assets, the actual value of which is difficult or impossible to determine, such as goodwill, copyrights, patents, trademarks, or leasehold improvements.

▶ *number of shares of common stock outstanding* means the sum of all common stock issues that are in the hands of shareholders.

Measure:

Book value is a measure of the relative worth of each dollar share of common stock issued by the company. It represents the amount of assets backing up each common share and gives some indication as to the safety of the shares and the accounting value that each represents.

Interpretation:

The higher this ratio, the better off common shareholders would be in the event of liquidation, though the liquidating value may be vastly different from the book value. Book value per share is sometimes compared against the market price of shares. A low book value per share of common stock can signal that the company has an insufficient amount of real assets standing behind its shares to fully repay common shareholders in the event of liquidation. However, a low book value could also indicate that the company has adopted extremely conservative accounting policies or invested quite heavily in intangible assets, such as research and development. Falling too low below a book value per share of common stock might make it difficult for the company to raise additional capital in the marketplace or through debt financing.

An unreasonably high book value per share may suggest that the accounting policies adopted by the company are extremely aggressive or that the company is running in a very efficient, profitable manner. One can determine this by examining what shape the activity and profitability ratios are in.

An increasing book value per share of common stock is generally a good sign in that the company is accumulating assets faster than it is accumulating debt or preferential stockholder obligations. On the other hand, a declining book value per share of common stock is generally not a good sign, though it may not be necessarily bad. For instance, if the reason the ratio is declining is because the company has just issued shares or is heavily engaged in successful research and development, then the decline may be entirely justifiable. However, if this is not the case, the company may be losing money from operations or may be writing down certain assets. Examining the annual report will help determine what is occurring.

Book value is often presumed to approximate liquidating value. However, the accounting policies adopted by the company and the price that a company may get for its assets during a "distress sale" accompanying liquidation may indeed be vastly different.

Example: Book Value Per Share of Common Stock

$$1988 = \frac{1{,}575{,}097 - 1{,}159{,}678}{111{,}670} = 3.72 \qquad\qquad 1987 = 6.91$$

or

$$1988 = \frac{1{,}575{,}097}{111{,}670} = 14.10 \qquad\qquad 1987 = 12.68$$

When examining the former calculation, Sara Lee experienced a dramatic drop in book value per share. The drop from 1987 to 1988 occurred because of the acquisition activity and consequent increase in intangible assets. When a company is acquired, the portion of the price paid for the company that cannot be attributed fully to real assets is treated as goodwill. Examining the latter calculation, an increase is found. This increase indicates that equity is being accumulated faster than debt.

---

   * This calculation is much more conservative than the second.
  ** A widely used ratio that is usually quoted in financial references.

NET ASSETS PER BOND

Data Source: Balance Sheet

$$\frac{\text{Net}}{\text{Assets} =} \quad \frac{\text{Total assets - Intangibles - All liabilities preceding bonds}}{\text{Number of bonds outstanding}}$$

Where:
  ▸ *total assets* means all assets owned by the company—whether they are currently being used or not—including current, fixed, sundry, and intangible assets.
  ▸ *intangibles* means all assets, the actual value of which is difficult or impossible to determine, such as goodwill, copyrights, patents, or leasehold improvements.
  ▸ *all liabilities preceding bonds* means all obligations of the company, such as taxes, that must be paid before debtholders receive any return on their investment in the event of the company's liquidation.
  ▸ *number of bonds outstanding* means the sum of all bond issues that are in the hands of bondholders.

Measure:
  Net assets per bond measures the amount of collateral standing behind the bonds issued by the company. It represents the number of dollars of assets backing up each bond, giving some indication of the bonds' safety.

Interpretation:
  Generally, the higher this ratio, the safer the bonds and the higher the likelihood that the company will have sufficient assets to return bondholders' principal in the event of liquidation. However, from a shareholder's point of view, an unreasonably high net asset per bond ratio can be a signal that the company is not using enough debt in its capital structure and therefore is using little leverage to maximize shareholder net worth.
  A low net asset per bond ratio can signal that the company does not have sufficient capital to repay bondholders in the event it were to terminate operations and begin dissolution. A company with too low a net asset value per bond may find it difficult to raise additional capital, or might have to pay significantly higher interest rates to get it.

An increasing net asset value per bond ratio may indicate that the company is accumulating assets faster than it is accumulating debt. A declining ratio may indicate that the company may be taking on debt faster than it is accumulating assets, which can be good or bad. On the one hand, it may be an effort by management to increase leverage for the benefit of shareholders, or it might indicate that the company is losing money from operations or is being forced to write down certain assets.

Example: Net Assets Per Bond

$$1988 = \frac{5,012,070 - 1,159,678 - 2,334,959^*}{877} = 1,730.25 \quad 1987 = 2,372.99$$

Sara Lee's decrease in asset per bond is somewhat dramatic but not unexpected. Again, Sara Lee's increase in intangible assets plays a large role in this coverage ratio. Even with the decrease, there is a comfortable cushion to cover the outstanding bonds. (Note that Sara Lee's balance sheet and income statements are reported in thousands; the bond ratio was also adjusted accordingly.)

* To compute this figure for Sara Lee, long term obligations under capital leases, deferred income taxes, and other liabilities are added to total current liabilities.

NET ASSETS PER PREFERRED SHARE

Data Source: Balance Sheet

$$\begin{array}{l}\text{Net Assets} \\ \text{Per Preferred} \\ \text{Share}\end{array} = \dfrac{\text{Total assets - Intangibles - Total debt}}{\text{Number of shares of preferred stock outstanding}}$$

Where:
  ► *total assets* means all assets owned by the company—whether they are currently being used or not—including current, fixed, sundry, and intangible assets.
  ► *intangibles* means all assets, the actual value of which is difficult or impossible to determine, such as goodwill, copyrights, patents, trademarks, or leasehold improvements.
  ► *total debt* means all obligations of the company, including current, fixed, and miscellaneous liabilities.
  ► *number of shares of preferred stock outstanding* means the sum of all preferred stock issues that are in the hands of shareholders.

Measure:
  Net assets per preferred share measures the amount of collateral standing behind the preferred shares issued by the company. It represents the number of dollars of assets backing up each preferred share, giving some indication about the safety of the preferred shares.

Interpretation:
  Generally, the higher this ratio, the safer each preferred share is and the higher the likelihood the company will have sufficient assets to return preferred shareholders' money in the event of liquidation. On the contrary, an unreasonably high net asset per share of preferred stock ratio can be a signal that the company is not using enough preferred in its capital structure and therefore has too little leverage to maximize shareholder net worth.
  A low net asset per share of preferred stock ratio can signal that the company does not have sufficient capital to repay preferred shareholders in the event it were to terminate operations and begin dissolution. Furthermore, a low ratio could make it difficult or more costly for the company to raise additional capital, especially through the sale of additional preferred shares. This in turn might force the

company to raise additional capital, through borrowing or through diluting common stock.

An increasing ratio may indicate that the company is accumulating assets faster than it is accumulating preferred equity. A declining net asset per share of preferred stock ratio may indicate that the company has just issued preferred shares, or, if this is not the case, the company may be losing money from operations or may be writing down certain assets. The annual report would indicate write-offs, if any.

Example: Net Assets Per Preferred Share

$$1988 = \frac{5,012,070 - 1,159,678 - 3,211,973}{1,501.5} = 426.52 \qquad 1987 = 993.97$$

In fiscal year 1988, Sara Lee issued 1,500 shares of preferred stock. On the surface that may seem like a small amount; however, the shares are redeemable for $100,000 per share versus $50 per share for the 1,500,000 other shares of preferred stock. The weighted average redeemable value per share therefore increases from $50 to $149. In either case, the collateral ratio is above the redeemable amount. (Note that because the other financial statement items are stated in thousands, the share figures have been divided by 1,000 to put them on parity with the other financial statement figures.)

COVERAGE MEASURES

Coverage measures examine a company's ability to meet its on-going financial obligations. They tell analysts how much of a cushion exists to meet these obligations, in the event income is reduced.

DIVIDEND PAYOUT

Data Source: Income Statement

$$\text{Dividend Payout} = \frac{\text{Common stock dividends paid}}{\text{Income available for common stock dividends}}$$

Where:
▶ *common stock dividends* paid means the total amount of money paid to common shareholders.
▶ *income available for common stock dividends* means the total amount of money that could be paid to common shareholders, calculated by subtracting preferred dividends and all unpaid by payable dividends from net income.

Measure:
Dividend payout ratio measures the percentage of distributable earnings distributed to common shareholders. It represents the percentage difference between the money the board of directors *is able to* distribute to common shareholders and what is *actually* distributed.

The board determines the payout ratio, which is typically based on its analysis of the company's working capital requirements, its future prospects, shareholder expectations, and the board's own desire for consistency.

Interpretation:
A frequently recurring low payout ratio can be a sign that the company has other uses for its investable funds than to pay them to shareholders. Specifically, companies that need additional money for working capital because of losses or marginal profitability, and companies that are using all of their excess cash to fund a program of rapid expansion, often have a low payout ratio. Some young and growing companies adopt low payout ratios because investors prefer

some dividends to *none at all.* This gives the company an opportunity to satisfy its need to retain capital and makes it easier for the board to maintain a constant dollar dividend payout despite the volatility in earnings so typical of younger, more growth-oriented companies.

A frequently recurring and unreasonably high payout ratio can be a sign that the company has little else to do with excess cash flow than to pay it to shareholders. Though shareholders may be happy to receive the cash, the effect on the company's growth rate may be detrimental, as money is not being retained to develop the company. However, if an unreasonably high payout ratio occurs, but has not previously occurred, it may be a sign that the company has had an exceptionally bad year but the board wishes to maintain a consistent dollar dividend payout.

An increasing dividend payout ratio can be a sign that the company is maturing and has less need for expansion or working capital. By the same token, an increasing dividend payout ratio is also a sign that the growth rate of the company may be slowing. It is quite typical for the board of directors to adopt a higher payout ratio as a company matures to inspirit shareholders for the use of their money, and to change the character of the company's securities by making them more attractive to conservative individuals and institutions.

Example: Dividend Payout

$$1988 = \frac{126,926}{315,681} = 0.40 \text{ or } 40\% \qquad\qquad 1987 = 0.39 \text{ or } 39\%$$

In 1988, Sara Lee paid out 40% of the net income available to common shareholders. This is a standard figure for such a mature company in a mature industry. The fact that it retained 59.79% of earnings shows that there is desire to invest in new ventures; its recent acquisitions are proof of this. Reading the annual report reveals the acquisition and divestive activities of a company.

FIXED CHARGE COVERAGE

Data Source: Income Statement

$$\text{Fixed Charge Coverage} = \frac{\text{Income before fixed charges and taxes}}{\text{Fixed charges}}$$

Where:

▶ *income before fixed charges and taxes* means income from all sources, less all the expenses associated with generating this income with the exception of interest charges, lease obligations, taxes, and extraordinary items.

▶ *fixed charges* means the interest payable on all of the company's fixed liabilities plus all payments on leaseholds. For Sara Lee, the interest figure can be found in the income statement. To determine the other fixed charges, one must read the notes to the financial statement in the annual report, which discloses fixed charges of $101,200 in 1988 ($97,200 in 1987).

Measure:

Fixed charge coverage measures the extent to which income covers the company's fixed charges. It represents how much of a revenue cushion the company has in order to meet its financial obligations to both debtholders and leaseholders.

Interpretation:

Generally, the higher this ratio, the more protected creditors and leaseholders are, the more stable the shareholders' position, and the easier it should be for the company to raise capital through borrowing. A high fixed charge coverage can signal that the company may not be adequately using the leverage effect of debt, and thereby not maximizing shareholder worth.

A low fixed charge coverage can signal a very aggressive management posture using potentially excessive amounts of leverage, or that the company is not earning an adequate return on borrowed capital or outstanding lease obligations.

A declining fixed charge coverage can signal anything from a decline in sales and profitability to an increase in the company's debtload, cost of debt, or lease obligations. Note, the interest rate a company pays on its debt can dramatically affect this ratio—

an increase in interest rates will cause a decline in fixed charge coverage.

Note: Despite its similarity to the interest coverage ratio, the fixed charge coverage ratio provides a more complete analysis because it includes virtually all the fixed charges a company is obligated to pay, not just the interest portion of these charges.

Example: Fixed Charge Coverage

$$1988 = \frac{734,461}{221,125} = 3.32 \qquad\qquad\qquad 1987 = 3.20$$

For 1988 Sara Lee's ability to pay its fixed charges was 3.32 times the actual fixed charges—a slight 0.12 increase over 1987. Sara Lee is in a good position to pay its fixed charges, even if there was a slight slump in sales.

INTEREST COVERAGE

Data Source: Income Statement

$$\text{Interest Coverage} = \frac{\text{Income before interest and taxes}}{\text{Interest}}$$

Where:
    ▸ *income before interest and taxes* means income from all sources less all the expenses associated with generating this income, with the exception of interest charges, taxes, and extraordinary items.
    ▸ *interest charges* means the interest payable on all of the company's fixed liabilities.

Measure:
    Interest coverage measures the extent to which income covers the company's interest requirements. It measures how much of a revenue cushion the company has in order to meet its financial obligations to debtholders.

Interpretation:
    The higher this ratio, the more protected the creditors are, the more stable the shareholders' position, and the easier it should be for the company to raise capital through borrowing. However, a high interest coverage coupled with low leverage can signal that the company may not be adequately using the leverage effects of debt, and thereby not maximizing shareholder wealth.
    A low interest coverage can signal a very aggressive management posture using potentially excessive amounts of leverage, or it can signal that the company is not earning an adequate return on the capital it has borrowed.
    A declining interest coverage can signal a decline in sales and profitability or an increase in the company's debtload or cost of debt. Note that the interest rate a company pays on its debt can dramatically affect this ratio inasmuch as an increase in interest rates will cause a decline in the interest coverage ratio.
    Note: though less complete than the fixed charge coverage, this ratio represents a reasonable method by which to judge how well the company is able to cover its costs of borrowing. Unfortunately, because many income statements do not break down fixed charges

in a fashion sufficient for a fixed charge coverage calculation to be made, the interest coverage ratio must often suffice.

Example: Interest Coverage

$$1988 = \frac{633,261}{119,925} = 5.28 \qquad\qquad 1987 = 5.24$$

As with its fixed charge coverage, Sara Lee's interest coverage increased in 1988. The income to cover interest payments is 5.28 times greater than the interest payments, a level high enough for debtholders to feel secure about receiving their payments, and also common shareholders to feel secure that debtholders will not be in a position to dictate what the company must do to meet its obligations.

PREFERRED DIVIDEND COVERAGE

Data Source: Income Statement

$$\text{Preferred Dividend Coverage} = \frac{\text{Net income}}{\text{Preferred dividends}}$$

Where:
> *net income* means net profit, the excess of all revenues less all expenses.
> *preferred dividends* means the total amount of money required to be paid to holders of the company's preferred shares.

Measure:
Preferred dividend coverage measures the extent to which income covers the company's preferred dividend requirements. It represents the amount of revenue cushion the company has in order to meet its financial obligations to preferred shareholders.

Interpretation:
The higher the preferred dividend coverage, the more protected and more stable the preferred shareholders' position. This ratio gives a good indication of the company's ability to earn and pay the dividends to preferred shareholders.

A high preferred dividend coverage can signal that the company may not be adequately using the leverage effect of debt and preferred equity, and common shareholders may not be earning the rate of return they could be earning. The higher the ratio, the easier it should be for the company to raise capital through borrowing. A declining preferred dividend coverage can signal a decline in sales and profitability.

A low preferred dividend coverage can signal a very aggressive management posture or that the company is too highly leveraged. It also could signal that the company is not earning an adequate return on borrowed capital or on the preferred equity it has raised.

Example: Preferred Dividend Coverage

$$1988 = \frac{325,075}{9,394} = 34.60 \qquad\qquad\qquad 1987 = 64.74$$

In 1988 Sara Lee's preferred dividend coverage dropped dramatically from 64.74 to 34.60. The drop came about because of the preferred stock issued in the 1988 fiscal year. Because 64.74 was a very high number, the drop to 34.60 should not sound any alarms. Net income has increased from $267,934 to $325,075, so a decrease in net income did not cause the drop. A level of 34.60 is still high, so preferred shareholders should not be concerned.

EARNINGS MEASURES

Earnings measures attempt to show how much money the company is making per share of common stock.

EARNINGS PER SHARE

Data Sources: Balance Sheet and Income Statement

$$\frac{\text{Earnings}}{\text{Per Share}} = \frac{\text{Net income - Preferred dividends}}{\text{Number of shares of common stock outstanding}}$$

Where:

▸ *net income* means net profit; the excess of all revenues less all expenses.

▸ *preferred dividends* means the total amount of money required to be paid to holders of the company's preferred shares.

▸ *number of shares of common stock outstanding* means the sum of all common stock issues that are in the hands of shareholders.

Measure:

Earnings per share measures the company's overall performance as it relates to common stock shareholders. It represents the amount of money each shareholder of common stock is entitled to and whether it is paid out in the form of dividends or reinvested in the company's future in the form of retained earnings.

Interpretation:

A low earnings per share figure indicates that the company is not making very much money. This can signal a number of things: the company may be inefficiently managed, it may have too many fixed obligations that need to be paid, or it may be heavily investing in research and development, while using overly conservative accounting policies.

Negative earnings per share indicate a company is actually losing money—shareholder equity is being used to keep the company operational. Negative or low earnings per share can make it difficult for a company to raise additional capital in the marketplace, either through debt or equity financing.

An unreasonably high earnings per share could indicate that the company may not be properly investing for the future—very little money is being spent on research and development, advertising, marketing, or infrastructure.

A declining earnings per share can signal a decline in profitability or an increase in the number of shares outstanding. It can also signal that the company is experiencing difficulties or, conversely, may be preparing for hard times by investing heavily in technology that has not yet begun to contribute to operating profits. Reading the annual report will tell whether the number of shares outstanding has changed or if the company's earnings are slowing down.

Example: Earnings Per Share

$$1988 = \frac{325{,}075 - 9{,}394}{111{,}670} = 2.83 \qquad\qquad 1987 = 2.35$$

In 1988, Sara Lee's earnings per share increased by 20%, outpacing the 14% increase in sales. The earnings increase above the sales increase can be accounted for by slight operational improvements and a decrease in the tax rate.

FULLY DILUTED EARNINGS PER SHARE

Data Sources: Balance Sheet and Income Statement

$$\begin{array}{l}\text{Fully} \\ \text{Diluted} \\ \text{Earnings} \\ \text{Per Share}\end{array} = \frac{\begin{array}{c}\text{Net} \\ \text{income}\end{array} + \begin{array}{c}\text{Convertible} \\ \text{preferred} \\ \text{dividends}\end{array} + \begin{array}{c}\text{Convertible} \\ \text{bond} \\ \text{interest}\end{array} - \begin{array}{c}\text{Interest tax} \\ \text{adjustment}\end{array}}{\begin{array}{l}\text{Number of shares of common stock outstanding} \\ \text{assuming conversion}\end{array}}$$

Where:

▶ *net income* means net profit; the excess of all revenues less all expenses.

▶ *convertible preferred dividends* means the total amount of money required to be paid to the holders of the company's preferred shares, which could be converted to common shares.

▶ *convertible bond interest* means the interest payable on all of the company's fixed liabilities, which could be converted to common shares.

▶ *interest tax adjustment* means any additional taxes that would result if the above-specified bond issues were converted and therefore the interest could no longer be deducted for tax purposes.

▶ *number of shares of common stock outstanding assuming conversion* means the sum of all common stock issues that would be in the hands of shareholders assuming that all of the company's convertible securities were converted to common shares.

Measure:

Fully diluted earnings per share is a measure of the company's overall performance as it relates to common shareholders and potential common shareholders. It represents the amount of money to which each shareholder of common stock is ultimately entitled and whether it is paid out in the form of dividends or reinvested in the form of retained earnings.

Interpretation:

A *low* fully diluted earnings per share figure indicates the company is not making very much money, and this can signal many problems: the company may be inefficiently run, it may have too many fixed obligations that need to be paid, or it may be investing too heavily in research and development while using overly conservative accounting policies. *Negative* fully diluted earnings per share indicate the company is losing money—shareholder equity is being used to keep the company operational. Negative or low fully diluted earnings per share can make it difficult for a company to raise additional capital in the marketplace.

Unreasonably high fully diluted earnings per share can indicate that the company may not be properly investing for the future. That is, very little money is being spent on such items as research and development, advertising, marketing, or infrastructure.

Declining fully diluted earnings per share can signal a decline in profitability or an increase in the number of shares outstanding. It can also signal that the company may be having hard times or, conversely, may be preparing for hard times by investing heavily in new technology that has not yet begun to contribute to operating profits. Reading the annual report will tell what the company is doing.

Example: Fully Diluted Earnings Per Share

$$1988 = \frac{315,681 + 4,547}{111,670 \ (+ 1,500)} = 2.83 \qquad\qquad 1987 = 2.35$$

In 1988 fully diluted earnings per share were the same as earnings per share. Therefore, common shareholders do not have to worry about the value of their holdings being diluted if the preferred shareholders convert their shares into common stock. Sara Lee does not hold any convertible bonds, so there is no convertible bond adjustment or tax adjustments. Dividends for common and preferred stocks are not tax deductible so they do not influence the tax adjustment in this computation.

PRIMARY EARNINGS PER SHARE

Data Sources: Balance Sheet and Income Statement

$$\text{Primary Earnings Per Share} = \frac{\text{Net income} + \text{Convertible (to common) preferred dividends} + \text{Convertible (to common) bond interest} - \text{Interest tax adjustment}}{\text{Number of shares of common stock outstanding assuming conversion}}$$

Where:
 ▸ *net income* means net profit; the excess of all revenues less all expenses.
 ▸ *convertible (to common) preferred dividends* means the total amount of money to be paid to holders of the company's preferred shares, which could be converted to common shares. They carry a dividend rate of two-thirds or less than the concurrent bank prime interest rate and would dilute ordinary earnings calculations by 3 percent or more if converted.
 ▸ *convertible (to common) bond interest* means the interest payable on all the company's fixed liabilities that could be converted to common shares. They carry an interest rate of two-thirds or less than the concurrent bank prime interest rate and would dilute ordinary earnings calculations by 3 percent or more if converted.
 ▸ *interest tax adjustment* means any additional taxes that would result if the above-specified bond issues were converted and whose interest could no longer be deducted for tax purposes.
 ▸ *number of shares of common stock outstanding assuming conversion* means the sum of all common stock issues that would be in the hands of shareholders, assuming that all convertible securities were converted to common shares.

Measure:
 Primary earnings per share is a measure of the company's overall performance as it relates to common shareholders and potential common shareholders. It represents the amount of money to which each share of common stock is entitled.

Interpretation:
 A low primary earnings per share figure indicates that the company is not making very much money. This can signal many

things: the company may be inefficiently run, it may have too many fixed obligations that need to be paid, or it may be investing too heavily in research and development while using overly conservative accounting policies. Negative primary earnings per share indicate the company is actually losing money—that is, shareholder equity is being used to keep the company operational. Negative or low primary earnings per share can make it difficult for a company to raise additional capital in the marketplace, either through debt or equity financing.

Unreasonably high primary earnings per share can indicate that the company may not be properly investing for the future. Specifically, it could mean that very little money is being spent on such items as research and development, advertising, marketing, or infrastructure.

Declining primary earnings per share can signal anything from a decline in profitability to an increase in the number of shares outstanding. It could signal that the company may be having hard times or, conversely, may be preparing for hard times by investing heavily in new technology that has not yet begun to contribute to operating profits.

Primary earnings per share differs from fully diluted earnings per share in that it only considers convertible securities that pay less than two-thirds of the going interest rate at the time of issue. This assumes that people are taking a below-market interest rate because they expect to make additional money when they convert their securities to common stock. Therefore, the chance of conversion is greater for these securities.

Example: Primary Earnings Per Share

$$1988 = \frac{325,075}{111,670} = 2.83 \qquad\qquad 1987 = 2.35$$

Sara Lee's convertible preferred securities interest payments are adjusted quarterly to match going rates and were not two-thirds below bank rates at the time of issue. Therefore, Sara Lee's primary earnings per share do not differ from its earnings per share.

LEVERAGE MEASURES

Leverage measures show how much debt is being used by the company relative to its assets and equity. It is important to know and follow this information because debt (financial leverage) can magnify return on equity during good times but create interest burdens when the company is suffering. In other words, if a company can earn more on its borrowings than it must pay to borrow, then financial leverage will serve to increase return on equity.

DEBT-TO-ASSETS

Data Source: Balance Sheet

$$\text{Debt-to-Assets} = \frac{\text{Total debt}}{\text{Total assets}}$$

Where:
- *total debt* means all obligations of the company, including current, fixed, and miscellaneous liabilities.
- *total assets* means all assets owned by the company—whether they are currently being used or not—including current, fixed, sundry, and intangible assets.

Measure:
Debt-to-asset's ratio measures the percentage of the company's funds provided by creditors. In other words, it measures the amount of financial leverage the company is using. Generally, companies with debt-to-asset percentages lower than 50 percent are considered to be well balanced in terms of leverage and risk, whereas ratios at or above 50 percent are thought to be using too much leverage and tend to be riskier.

Interpretation:
The more debt a company has, the higher its interest costs will be. The leverage effect of debt is beneficial if a company can earn returns higher than its cost of interest on the borrowed funds. If it can't, the effect of leverage is detrimental. Essentially, the leverage effect of debt tends to magnify the returns a company generates on its invested assets.

Typically, high leverage translates into more volatile earnings. The higher the ratio, the higher the company's earnings volatility, the higher its risk and the greater the potential rate of return for shareholders.

Typically, the lower this ratio, the more stable a company's earnings, the less risk the shares carry, and the lower the expected rate of return for shareholders. Creditors, debtholders, and preferred shareholders prefer companies with low debt-to-assets ratios because there tends to be less chance of defaulting on outstanding loans, and a higher percentage of assets to repay loans in the unlikely event of default.

A declining ratio can indicate anything from the company's increase in stability to management's insufficient use of leverage. This can be determined by looking at the relative level of the ratio (above or below 50). If the company is above 50 percent, a declining debt-to-assets ratio can be looked upon as becoming more stable. However, if the ratio was below 50 percent to begin with, a declining ratio may indicate that the company may not be making enough use of leverage.

Example: Debt-to-Assets

$$1988 = \frac{3,211,973}{5,012,070} = 0.64 \text{ or } 64\% \qquad\qquad 1987 = 0.64 \text{ or } 64\%$$

On the surface, Sara Lee's debt-to-assets ratio seems high. However, Sara Lee is in a good position to take on debt without exposing its debtholders to a large risk of default. Further, since Sara Lee is generating a substantial cash flow and has no trouble paying its interest and fixed charges —fixed charge coverage is 3.3 and interest coverage is 5.3—this supports the conclusion that Sara Lee can well afford its debt structure. Therefore, it seems reasonable that Sara Lee has increased its debt-to-assets ratio to provide the financial benefits of leverage.

DEBT-TO-EQUITY

Data Source: Balance Sheet

$$\text{Debt-to-Equity} \quad = \quad \frac{\text{Funded debt}}{\text{Shareholders' equity}}$$

Where:
▸ *funded debt* means all long-term obligations of the company that will mature in five years or more.
▸ *shareholders' equity* means the total equity investment in the company, including preferred stock, common stock, paid-in capital, and retained earnings.

Measure:
Debt-to-equity measures the percentage of the company's funds provided by creditors. It measures the effects of leverage on shareholder money. Usually, 100 percent or more is construed to be a high debt-to-equity ratio.

Interpretation:
From an earnings perspective, high debt translates into high interest charges. The leverage effect is beneficial if the company can earn returns higher than the cost of interest on borrowed funds. If it doesn't, the leverage effect is detrimental. Essentially, leverage magnifies the returns earned on shareholder assets.

Typically, high leverage translates into more volatile earnings. The higher the debt-to-equity ratio, the higher the company's risk and the greater the potential rate of return for shareholders.

The lower this ratio, the more stable a company's earnings, the less risk the shares carry, and the lower the expected rate of return for shareholders. Creditors, debtholders, and preferred shareholders all prefer companies with low debt-to-equity ratios.

A declining ratio can indicate anything from the company becoming more stable to a declining use of leverage by management. This can be determined by looking at the relative level of the ratio.

Example: Debt-to-Equity

$$1988 = \frac{893,434}{1,800,097} = 0.50 \text{ or } 50\% \qquad\qquad 1987 = 0.42 \text{ or } 42\%$$

A 50% debt-to-equity ratio may seem low, but one should also look at the debt-to-asset ratio. Sara Lee's debt-to-asset ratio showed that 64% of all assets were financed by debt, yet capitalized debt is only 57% of equity. This tells us that in the past Sara Lee financed a lot of its assets with short-term debt, which is usually not a good course of action. This is why the debt-to-equity increase from 42% to 50% should be welcomed, not looked down upon.

LIQUIDITY MEASURES

Liquidity measures examine how easily companies can pay off their short-term obligations.

CASH (or LIQUIDITY)

Data Source: Balance Sheet

$$\text{Cash} = \frac{\text{Cash on hand in bank + Marketable securities}}{\text{Current liabilities}}$$

Where:
 ► *cash on hand in bank* means currency and currency equivalents.
 ► *marketable securities* means U.S. government securities, bankers' acceptances, commercial paper, and corporate securities, valued at market rather than at cost.
 ► *current liabilities* means items that must be paid within the current year, such as accounts payable, accrued expenses, accrued and withheld taxes, unearned revenues, notes payable, dividends payable, and the current maturities of long-term debts.

Measure:
 Cash ratio measures how easily a company can pay off its short-term liabilities.

Interpretation:
 Cash ratio, though less frequently used than the current ratio or quick asset ratio, gives a more critical analysis of the company's cash position. The cash ratio is especially well suited for evaluating companies in cash-intensive industries.
 A company with too low a cash ratio may be in danger of running out of the funds necessary to keep going during an economic downturn, may fall behind on payments for raw materials and be forced to halt production, or may have to delay an advertising campaign, which could disrupt its marketing efforts.
 An unreasonably high cash ratio could suggest anything from an overly conservative management stance to a company that is seeking a takeover or is a takeover target itself. By examining other companies one can help determine the appropriate levels.

A declining cash ratio is generally not a good sign, though quite often companies in seasonal industries will accumulate cash during certain times and spend cash during other times.

Example: Cash

$$1988 = \frac{178,552}{1,806,161} = 0.10 \qquad\qquad 1987 = 0.19$$

Sara Lee's cash ratio decreased substantially during the year. With a ratio of 0.10 it would only be able to pay off 10% of its current liabilities with cash. In order to pay off its current liabilities, Sara Lee would have to sell its inventory, probably below its market value, and collect on its accounts receivable, which takes time (over 25 days in Sara Lee's case—see average collection period ratio), or borrow funds which may be both difficult and costly.

CURRENT (or WORKING) CAPITAL

Data Source: Balance Sheet

$$\text{Current Capital} = \frac{\text{Current assets}}{\text{Current liabilities}}$$

Where:
▶ *current assets* means items that either represent cash or will be or could be converted into cash in a relatively short period of time, such as cash, marketable securities (valued at cost), accounts receivable, notes receivable, inventory, and prepaid expenses.
▶ *current liabilities* means items that must be paid within the current year, such as accounts payable, accrued expenses, accrued and withheld taxes, unearned revenues, notes payable, dividends payable, and the current maturities of long-term debts.

Measure:
Current or working capital ratio tests the company's ability to raise cash to meet its current liabilities.

Interpretation:
The higher this ratio, the easier it will be for the company to meet its short-term financial obligations. For many years, 2.0 and higher was considered a minimum current ratio for a healthy company. However, as more sophisticated cash management techniques have been developed, companies are able to keep less cash on hand, and therefore the level has dropped.

The current capital ratio should be examined in conjunction with the company's other measures and the industry in general. The level of the current ratio depends on industry factors because the numerator of the equation includes both inventory and accounts receivable (the inventory may be perishable, subject to obsolescence, or otherwise not readily salable, and the accounts receivable may be aging and potentially uncollectible).

A low current capital ratio can be a signal that the company may be in danger of running out of funds or at the very least, may be having difficulties paying its bills. The reasons for this are simple: the timely payment of current liabilities depends on the company's cash reserves, its timely receipt of cash from receivables, and its ability to quickly convert other current assets into cash.

Too high a ratio could suggest anything from an overly conservative management stance to a company that is seeking a takeover or is a takeover target itself. Reading analysts' reports might help determine what actually is happening.

A declining current capital ratio is generally not a good sign, though quite often companies in seasonal industries will accumulate cash during certain times and spend cash during other times.

Example: Current Capital

$$1988 = \frac{2,088,872}{1,806,161} = 1.16 \qquad\qquad 1987 = 1.23$$

Sara Lee's current capital ratio is well below the old norm of 2.0; however, it is in line with its level in the 1980s and not too dissimilar to the current ratios of other food companies. The food industry tends to be fairly stable, thus allowing food companies to have lower current ratios.

QUICK ASSET (or ACID TEST)

Data Source: Balance Sheet

$$\text{Quick Asset} = \frac{\text{Total current assets - Inventory - Prepaid expenses}}{\text{Current liabilities}}$$

Where:
▶ *total current assets* means those items that either represent cash or will or could be converted into cash in a relatively short period of time, including cash, marketable securities (valued at cost), accounts receivable, notes receivable, inventory, and prepaid expenses.

▶ *inventory* means raw materials, work in progress, and finished merchandise waiting for sale, valued at the lower of cost or market value.

▶ *prepaid expenses* means payments or deposits made in anticipation of the receipt of goods or services that will be used at some point in the future. (This item is not available in Sara Lee's balance sheet.)

▶ *current liabilities* means items that must be paid within the current year, including accounts payable, accrued expenses, accrued and withheld taxes, unearned revenues, notes payable, dividends payable, and the current maturities of long-term debts.

Measure:
Quick asset ratio tests the company's ability to raise cash in a temporary financial crisis.

Interpretation:
The higher this ratio, the easier it will be for the company to raise cash in an emergency. *Too high* a ratio can suggest anything from an overly conservative management stance to a company seeking a takeover or becoming a takeover target.

A low quick asset ratio can signal that the company may be in danger of running out of funds or at the very least, may be having financial difficulties—that is, the company may be having trouble paying its bills. The reasons behind this are simple: the timely payment of current liabilities depends on the company's cash reserves, its timely receipt of cash from its receivables, and its ability to convert other current assets into cash.

A declining quick asset ratio is generally not a good sign; however, companies in seasonal industries may accumulate cash during certain times and spend cash at other times.

Note: the quick asset ratio should be examined in conjunction with liability and activity measures. The level of the ratio is often dependent on the kind of business the company is in and the general economic condition of the industry.

Example: Quick Asset

$$1988 = \frac{2{,}088{,}872 - 1{,}127{,}453}{1{,}806{,}161} = 0.53 \qquad\qquad 1987 = 0.59$$

As with other liquidity measures, the quick asset ratio is a bit low, but the company is in a good general financial position. It is generating plenty of cash flow to meet its obligations and is in a stable industry.

PROFITABILITY MEASURES

Profitability measures attempt to assess the profitability of a company. This method also allows for comparison over time and with other companies.

OPERATING (or EXPENSE)

Data Source: Income Statement

$$\text{Operating} = \frac{\text{Cost of goods sold} + \text{Operating expenses}}{\text{Net sales}}$$

Where:
  ▶ *cost of goods sold* means the cost of the inventory sold during the period.
  ▶ *operating expenses* means all of the other expenses associated with operating the company, including selling and administrative expenses, and depreciation.
  ▶ *net sales* means gross sales, less any discounts, returns, and refunds.

Measure:
  Operating ratio measures the company's operating efficiency. It compares the total expenses associated with sales to the revenue generated by those sales.

Interpretation:
  A low operating ratio can signal a highly efficient operation and exceptionally effective management. On the other hand, it can signal that the company is using overly conservative accounting policies or is spending insufficient money on research and development. If a company's sales are not increasing greatly, yet the dividend payout ratio is, then the company may be entering the mature stage and management is choosing to give the money to shareholders, rather than using it to grow.
  A high operating ratio can signal general inefficiency or ineffective management. Such a situation can also indicate that a company uses extremely aggressive accounting policies, is spending

too much on research and development, or does not have enough sales to justify its infrastructure.

An increasing operating ratio can signal aging property, plant, and equipment; declining sales volume; declining overall efficiency; or inappropriate policy making.

Note: This ratio is the complement of the profit margin ratio—they will always total 100 percent.

Example: Operating

$$1988 = \frac{7,096,756 + 2,717,504}{10,423,816} = 94.15\% \qquad\qquad 1987 = 94.36\%$$

Sara Lee's operating ratio decreased very slightly from 1987 to 1988. Because an operating ratio shows what percentage of sales covers operating costs, a decline in the operating ratio is positive. While this ratio seems high, the food industry is known for low profit margins (which translates into high operating ratios) and quick turnover to make money. Actually, Sara Lee's ratio is better than the industry's ratio, which had an average of 95.7% in 1988 and 96.0% in 1987.

PROFIT MARGIN

Data Source: Income Statement

$$\text{Profit Margin} = \frac{\text{Operating income}}{\text{Net sales}}$$

Where:
  ► *operating income* means gross sales less any discounts, returns, and refunds, less the cost of these sales, all selling and administrative expenses, and depreciation.
  ► *net sales* means gross sales, less any discounts, returns, and refunds.

Measure:
Profit margin ratio is a measure of the company's operating efficiency. It is a measure of the percentage contribution to operating income that each dollar of sales generates, expressed on a pre-tax basis.

Interpretation:
The higher the profit margin, the more efficiently the firm is operating. However, an unreasonably high profit margin ratio can be a signal of a highly efficient operation and exceptionally effective management; *or* it could signal that the company is using overly conservative accounting policies or spending insufficient money on research and development.

A low profit margin ratio can be a signal of general inefficiency or ineffective management, or that a company is using extremely aggressive accounting policies, is spending too much on research and development, or does not have enough sales to justify its infrastructure.

A declining profit margin can signal aging property, plant, and equipment; declining sales volume; declining overall efficiency; or inappropriate management policy making. By tracking each individual element, a diagnosis can be made.

Note: This ratio is the complement of the operating ratio—they will always total 100 percent.

Example: Profit Margin

$$1988 = \frac{609,556}{10,423,816} = 5.85\% \qquad\qquad 1987 = 5.64\%$$

Sara Lee did not provide a gross sales level, so operating income was computed by taking net sales (which already subtracted discounts, returns, and refunds) and subtracting cost of goods sold, and selling, general, and administrative expenses. Sara Lee's profit margin increased slightly between 1987 and 1988. It remains above average for the food processing industry, which Value Line shows as 4.3% for 1988 (4.0% for 1987).

RETURN ON ASSETS

Data Sources: Balance Sheet and Income Statement

Two commonly used methods:

$$\text{Return on Assets} = \frac{\text{Net income}}{\text{Total assets}}$$

or

$$\text{Return on Assets} = \frac{\text{Net income}}{\text{Net sales}} \times \frac{\text{Net sales}}{\text{Total assets}} \quad *$$

Where:
 ▸ *net income* means net profit; the excess of all revenues less all expenses.
 ▸ *total assets* means all assets owned by the company—whether they are currently being used or not—including current, fixed, sundry, and intangible assets.
 ▸ *net income/net sales* means net income divided by sales.
 ▸ *net sales/total assets* means sales divided by total assets (total asset turnover).
 ▸ *net sales* means gross sales, less discounts, returns, and refunds.

Measure:
 Return on assets tests the efficiency of the company's use of its assets. It is a measure of the company's ability to earn profits on its asset base.

Interpretation:
 Generally, the higher the return on assets ratio, the more efficiently the company is operating. A high return on assets can signal a highly efficient operation and exceptionally effective management, or it can signal overly conservative accounting policies or insufficient spending on research and development.
 This ratio is similar to the return on invested capital and the return on equity ratios. By its very nature, a high return on assets translates into a still higher return on equity, because the numerator of both equations is the same and the denominator of the former must be equal to or greater than that of the latter.

A low return on assets ratio can signal a company with inefficient operations or ineffective management; or it can result from extremely aggressive accounting policies, significant expenditures on research and development, or insufficient sales to justify the company's infrastructure.

A declining return on assets can signal a weakening company, declining sales volume, declining overall efficiency, or inappropriate policy making.

Example: Return on Assets

$$1988 = \frac{325{,}075}{5{,}012{,}070} = 6.49\% \qquad\qquad 1987 = 6.37\%$$

or

$$1988 = \frac{325{,}075}{10{,}423{,}816} \times \frac{10{,}423{,}816}{5{,}012{,}070} = 6.49\% \qquad\qquad 1987 = 6.37\%$$

Sara Lee's return on assets increased very slightly for 1988. The increase, though slight, is good to see because of Sara Lee's increase in size.

---

* Looking at return on assets by first taking net income over sales and multiplying the results by net sales over total assets helps to show that return on assets is affected by both efficient use of assets and by having a good profit margin on sales.

RETURN ON EQUITY

Data Sources: Balance Sheet and Income Statement

Two commonly used methods:

$$\text{Return on Equity} = \frac{\text{Net income}}{\text{Shareholders' equity}}$$

or

$$\text{Return on Equity} = \frac{\text{Return on assets (investments)}}{(1 - \text{Total debt/Total assets})} \ *$$

Where:
    ► *net income* means net profit; the excess of all revenues less all expenses.
    ► *shareholders' equity* means the total equity investment in the company, including preferred stock, common stock, paid-in capital, and retained earnings.
    ► *return on assets* means the net income divided by the total assets.
    ► *total debt/total assets* means the total debt divided by the total assets.
    ► *total debt* means all obligations of the company, including current, fixed, and miscellaneous liabilities.
    ► *total assets* means all assets owned by the company—whether they are currently being used or not—including current, fixed, sundry, and intangible assets.

Measure:
    Return on equity tests the efficiency of the company's use of its equity capital. It is a measure of the company's ability to earn profits on shareholder equity.

Interpretation:
    This ratio is the cornerstone of the financial analysis process, because it is management's express responsibility to maximize this ratio. Generally, the higher the return on equity ratio, the more efficiently the company is operating and the better the return available to shareholders.

An unreasonably high return on equity can signal a highly efficient operation or exceptionally effective management. Or it could signal overly conservative accounting policies, a great deal of financial leverage, or insufficient spending on research and development. When examining return on equity, examine both the profit margin and the degree of financial leverage to determine what is the driving force behind the return on equity.

A low return on equity ratio can signal a company with inefficient operations or ineffective management. Or it could result from extremely aggressive accounting policies, significant expenditures on research and development, insufficient sales to justify the company's infrastructure, or little debt in a company's capital structure.

A declining return on equity can signal a weakening company, declining sales volume, declining overall efficiency, inappropriate policy making, or a decrease in the company's debt load.

Example: Return on Equity

$$1988 = \frac{325,075}{1,800,097} = 18.06\% \qquad\qquad 1987 = 17.64\%$$

or

$$1988 = \frac{6.49\%}{1 - \frac{3,211,973}{5,012,070}} = 18.06\% \qquad\qquad 1987 = 17.64\%$$

Sara Lee's return on equity increased in 1988 despite a slight decrease in financial leverage. The return on equity is good but lags slightly behind the food processing industry, which *Value Line* reported as 19.0% for 1988 (18.1% for 1987).

---

* Looking at return on equity by dividing return on assets by one minus the total debt to total assets ratio highlights how debt can be used to increase return on equity. The return on equity is a function of making good use of assets and careful use of debt. Debt will increase the return on equity, but too much debt may hurt the company if the company cannot meet its interest payments and thereby defaults.

RETURN ON INVESTED CAPITAL

Data Sources: Balance Sheet and Income Statement

$$\text{Return on Invested Capital} = \frac{\text{Net income} + \text{Interest on funded debt}}{\text{Total capitalization}}$$

Where:
 ▸ *net income* means net profit; the excess of all revenues less all expenses.
 ▸ *interest on funded debt* means the interest payable on all the company's fixed liabilities.
 ▸ *total capitalization* means all fixed liabilities and shareholders' equity; in essence, the total long-term investment in the company from all sources.

Measure:
 Return on invested capital measures the company's efficiency of use of capital. It tests the productivity of the company's long-term invested capital.

Interpretation:
 The higher this ratio, the better the company is managing its operations and the more profitably it is employing capital. An unreasonably high return on invested capital can signal a highly efficient operation and exceptionally effective management, or it could indicate overly conservative accounting policies or insufficient spending on research and development.
 This ratio is similar to the return on assets and the return on equity ratios. However, a high return on invested capital does not necessarily translate into a high return on assets or a high return on equity, as this ratio excludes the effects of interest by adding interest expense back to net income. Therefore, a company could have a high return on invested capital yet have a low (or negative) return on equity or assets.
 A low return on invested capital can signal a company with inefficient operations or ineffective management. However, such a situation also could result from extremely aggressive accounting policies, significant expenditures on research and development, or insufficient sales to justify the company's infrastructure. By reading

the annual report and examining sales and research and development expenditures, a better determination can be made.

A declining return on invested capital can signal a weakening company, declining sales volume, declining overall efficiency, or inappropriate policy making.

Example: Return on Invested Capital

$$1988 = \frac{325,075 + 119,925}{3,205,909*} = 13.88\% \qquad\qquad 1987 = 14.35\%$$

Sara Lee experienced a slight decline in its return on invested capital ratio for 1988. It had a 23% increase in invested capital but only a 19.4% increase in net income plus interest. Sara Lee's return on invested capital is still at a good level but should be watched closely.

* Sara Lee's total capitalization includes its long-term debt, long-term obligations under capital leases, deferred income taxes, and other liabilities. A quick way to compute this is to subtract total current liabilities from total assets.

DU PONT ANALYSIS

Ratio analysis provides a great deal of information about how a company is performing and how it is structured. However, examining the ratios individually makes it difficult to see how they interact or how they impact on the stockholder. *Du Pont analysis* is a method used to examine how the various financial ratios interact. The return a company provides on shareholder funds is a key considera- tion. Du Pont analysis provides a framework showing how the company's operation and its financing affect the return on equity. Du Pont analysis derives its name from the Du Pont corporation, which developed this approach in the early 1920s.

Figure 2.5 diagrams the Du Pont analysis for Sara Lee. The top half of the chart deals primarily with the income statement, while the bottom half emphasizes the balance sheet. This separation highlights the fact that return on equity is affected by firm profit- ability and balance sheet structure.

Sales, cost of goods sold, selling and administration expenses, interest expense, interest income (other income), and taxes are entered from the income statement to determine net income. Net income divided by sales produces Sara Lee's after-tax profit margin of 3.1 percent.

Asset data from the balance sheet is entered to determine the total assets. Other assets include trademarks, investments in uncon- solidated companies, and intangibles. Dividing sales by total assets provides the asset turnover ratio of 2.1. Asset turnover multiplied by profit margin provides a return on assets of 6.5 percent for Sara Lee.

Liabilities from the balance sheet are entered to determine the total debt. Other current assets consist of notes payable, current maturities of long-term debt, and current obligations under capital leases. Other liabilities include long-term obligations under capital leases, deferred income taxes and "other liabilities" listed on the balance sheet. Total debt divided by total assets provides a financial leverage figure of 64.1 percent. Financial leverage is the percentage of assets financed through debt.

Dividing return on assets of 6.5 percent by 1, less 64.1 percent (financial leverage) gives a return on equity of 18.1 percent. For 1988 Sara Lee's shareholders had a return of 18.1 percent for their equity interest in the company.

Examining the interplay between the ratios is the key behind Du Pont analysis. Return on equity can be increased by a higher return on assets or a higher degree of leverage—more debt relative to assets. The high degree of financial leverage is how buy-out artists

Figure 2.5. Du Pont Analysis—Sara Lee Corporation

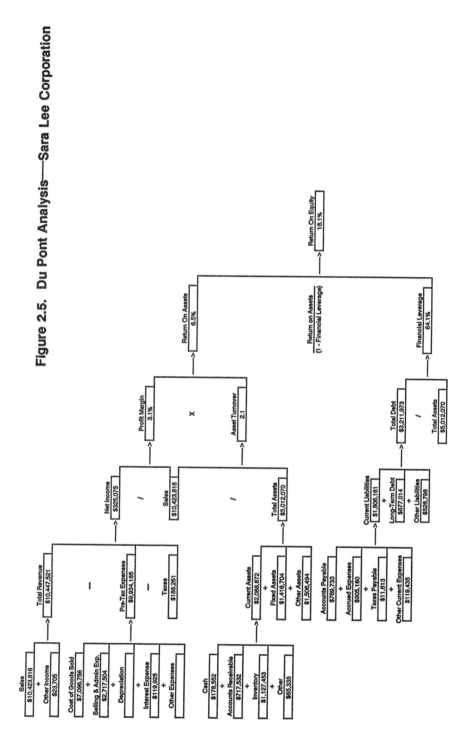

hope to profit when they take on huge amounts of debt in acquiring companies. The risk in the strategy is that the company will not generate enough cash flow to cover the interest payments. Examining leverage in this regard shows that proper use of financial leverage can help increase the return on equity. If Sara Lee had no debt, its return on equity would be the same as its return on assets, 6.5 percent.

Return on assets in turn can be increased with higher profit margins or higher asset turnover. Margins are improved by lowering expenses relative to sales. The profit margin calculation differs in the Du Pont analysis from the operating profit margin ratio presented earlier because it takes other income, interest expense, and taxes into account. Asset turnover can be improved by selling more goods with a given level of assets. This is why firms try to divest assets (operations) that do not generate sales or are decreasing their sales generation.

Du Pont analysis highlights the interaction between the operations of companies and the methods of financing used in those operations. It helps to remind analysts that each ratio should be examined to see how it impacts on the overall organization, as well as the shareholders.

3 / FUNDAMENTAL ANALYSIS AND MARKET VALUATION

OVERVIEW

Of all the facets of fundamental analysis, evaluating market multipliers deals the most with factors external to the company. In many ways, evaluating market multipliers approaches technical analysis in that it is based on estimating how the changing perceptions of the investing public will translate into the public's willingness to pay more or less for a specific security or groups of securities.

As discussed in "Life Cycle Analysis," market multipliers are a measure of investors' willingness to buy the future stream of income that is part and parcel to the ownership of a company. As changes occur in the economy, the industry, and the company, investors' willingness to own these streams of income also changes. As actual changes occur in investors' *perceptions* of the economy, the industry, and the company, so too will their valuation of a company's securities.

Methodology used to evaluate changes in market multipliers ranges from the simplistic approach of ignoring any changes and just using last year's numbers, to much more sophisticated approaches that employ trend analysis and growth rate models of the economy and the company. Many of these techniques are proprietary, and most require significant computing power and databases from which to draw information.

However, a company's market valuation can be calculated by using data from the balance sheet, the income statement, and the stock transaction pages of the local newspaper. *Market valuation* is comprised of multipliers that investors are willing to apply to the company's earnings and dividends to arrive at the price they are willing to pay for the securities in the open market. This is determined by the dividend yield and price-earnings ratios.

These measures are then compared against other measures for the same company, compared against themselves over time, and compared against other companies within the same industry, to determine the worthiness of the company's securities.

MARKET VALUATION RATIOS

Market valuation ratios compare company factors with the market price to provide comparison statistics and valuation figures.

DIVIDEND YIELD

Data Sources: Balance Sheet, Income Statement, and Marketplace

$$\text{Dividend Yield} = \frac{\text{Annual per share dividend}}{\text{Price per share}}$$

Where:
 ▸ *annual per share dividend* means the amount of dividend to be paid on each share of the company's stock.
 ▸ *price per share* means the current market price of each share as determined by buyers and sellers in the marketplace.

Measure:
Dividend yield is a measure of the cash yield investors earn for investing in the shares of the company. It represents the percentage cash return that a stockholder receives.

Interpretation:
Typically, the higher the yield, the safer the investment, and the less growth-oriented the stock. However, a very high dividend yield can suggest that the company is unable to identify any suitable investment opportunities within or outside its industry suggesting the company may be facing much slower growth prospects. Or, it could simply mean that shareholders are being rewarded for their investments. A high dividend yield associated with a dramatic fall in stock price may indicate that the dividend rate will be cut or that the shares are underpriced in the market.

A low dividend yield can signal that the company retains earnings as a source of investable funds, or that the company is earning an insufficient return on invested assets. A low dividend yield associated with a dramatic rise in stock price may be a sign that the dividend rate, set by the board of directors, is about to be increased or that the stock shares are overpriced.

An increasing dividend yield caused by an increasing annual dividend rate (the numerator) shows that the board of directors feels comfortable enough with the company's future to reward its shareholders more heavily. Conversely, a declining dividend yield caused by a declining numerator suggests that the board of directors is willing to risk shareholder disenchantment by lowering the dividend rate.

Example: Dividend Yield

$$1988 = \frac{1.15}{36.875*} = 3.12\% \qquad\qquad 1987 = 2.04\%$$

Like many stocks, Sara Lee experienced a dramatic increase in dividend yield. In 1987 the market experienced the largest single-day decrease in history. In general, the market environment accounts for the decrease in Sara Lee's stock price from $46.5 to $36.875. However, during the year Sara Lee also had a hefty dividend increase of 21%, from $0.95 to $1.15. The combination of the dividend increase and stock price decline explains the 55% increase in the dividend yield.

*Sara Lee's stock price on July 2, 1988, its fiscal year end.

PRICE-EARNINGS

Data Sources: Balance Sheet, Income Statement, and Marketplace

$$\text{Price-Earnings} = \frac{\text{Price per share}}{\text{Earnings per share}}$$

Where:

▶ *price per share* means the current market price of each share as determined by buyers and sellers in the marketplace.

▶ *earnings per share* (or sometimes, as in Sara Lee's income statement, referred to as "net income per common share") means the amount of money each shareholder is ultimately entitled to, whether it is paid out or retained.

Measure:

Price-earnings ratio is a measure of the value that investors place on the company's earnings. It represents the amount of money investors are willing to pay *today* for the future stream of benefits that they expect to get from an investment in the company's shares, including dividends, their "portion" of retained earnings, and share price appreciation.

Interpretation:

Typically, the higher the price-earnings ratio, the riskier, more volatile the investment. An unreasonably high price-earnings ratio or one that is "not meaningful" is a sign that investors perceive the company to be extremely risky, expect the company to experience a turnaround or explosive growth in earnings, or, for one reason or another, have become enamored with the stock. "Not meaningful" price-earnings ratios result when a company does not have any earnings or is losing money. In these situations, the ratio is not meaningful because the divisor of the equation (earnings per share) is a "zero" or a negative number.

A low price-earnings ratio can be a signal that investors regard the company as a conservative, safety-oriented investment; expect the company's earnings to drop or its growth rate of earnings to slow; have little confidence in the company's reported earnings or earnings trend; or expect the industry or economy as a whole to perform poorly. Typically, older, safer, more mature companies have lower price-earnings ratios than do young, faster-growing, riskier companies.

An increasing price-earnings ratio is generally a good sign. Increasing price-earnings ratios should be caused by increases in prices outpacing earnings gains, not decreasing earnings.

Contrary to what might otherwise be expected, some investment strategies concentrate on buying the shares of those companies with low price-earnings ratios (presumed undervalued) and short-selling those with ratios that are unreasonably high (presumed overvalued).

Price-earnings ratios can be calculated using historical earnings per share data or expected earnings per share data. When historical data is used, the price-earnings ratio is said to be trailing. Price-earnings ratios calculated using the next year's expected earnings are said to be normalized.

Example: Price-Earnings

$$1988 = \frac{36.875}{2.83} = 13.03 \qquad\qquad 1987 = 19.78$$

Sara Lee's price-earnings ratio declined dramatically—34%—from 19.78 to 13.03. Using data from The S&P Outlook, a service that trades and reports on the market, the S&P 500 experienced a similar 32% drop from 16.8 to 11.4. During this time period earnings per share increased. Thus, the drop was not due to earnings decrease but rather to a general decline in market prices.

STOCK SCREENING AND EVALUATION

One of the reasons for analyzing a company's financial condition is to determine the intrinsic value of its stock: what is the stock really worth. Because the value of a company most often is based on future earnings, investors must attempt to forecast the company's *future earnings potential* before making a buy-sell decision.

Determining a company's future earnings potential can be accomplished by using historical data and applying one of the two market valuation ratios previously discussed. The price-earnings ratio of a company over a period of time can be used for companies with low or non-existent dividends—typical growth or aggressive growth companies. The dividend yield ratio is used when analyzing high dividend paying companies—more mature companies. However, even a high dividend paying company should have earnings-based analysis performed in order to examine the company's ability to *continue* paying high dividends. After all, earnings provide cash for the dividends.

Both valuation methods assume that the historical performance of a security is a logical basis for estimating the future performance. The market valuation measures, along with the financial ratios discussed in previous sections, can be compared against similar companies, the industry, and the market as a whole to get a sense of the company's overall financial status.

Figure 3.1, on pages 90 and 91, provides a worksheet to systematically determine whether a company or stock is properly valued. Both the price-earnings and dividend yield approaches are included. The following discussion explains how to complete the stock screening worksheet and ends with an example using data from the Sara Lee Corporation.

STOCK SCREENING WORKSHEET

Section I—Stock History

This information can be gathered from *Value Line Industry Survey* or the *S&P's Stock Reports*. The standard one-page listing of a company in *Value Line* provides a wealth of data that will give all the necessary information to make an analysis. Obtaining the high and low prices, earnings per share, and dividends per share from *Value Line* is direct and straight-forward. Return on equity (ROE) can be calculated by using one of the two ratios discussed in the previous section. Or, a calculated ROE can be found in *Value Line*

Industry Survey listed under *% earned on net worth* or in *S&P's Stock Reports* listed under ROE.

This data is used to calculate the price-earnings and dividend yield historical data. The high and low P/E ratios are *trailing* figures, calculated for each year by dividing the high price by earnings per share (EPS) to obtain the high P/E ratios. Conversely, to obtain the low P/E ratios, the low prices are divided by the EPSs.

A slightly different method is used to calculate the dividend yield history. To get a low dividend yield, the dividend is divided by the high price; to get a high dividend yield, the dividend is divided by the low price. The figures obtained in this section will be used to estimate the range of value in Section IV.

Section II—Market and Industry Data

Market and industry data can be obtained from the *S&P's Industry Surveys*, *Value Line Industry Survey* or other publications such as *Barron's*. To calculate long-term debt-to-equity, long-term debt is divided by net worth. The information in this section provides the basis for industry and market comparisons.

Section III—Financial Checklist

There are five parts to this section. Part A measures the company's ability to earn profits on shareholder equity. A high and stable ROE indicates that the company is using its equity capital productively and therefore is operating efficiently.

Part B, long-term debt-to-equity, measures the effects of leverage on shareholder money. The data for this ratio, also found in *Value Line*, is calculated by dividing current long-term debt by current equity (net worth). This ratio and the current price-earnings ratio (Part C) are then compared against industry norms.

Part D of the Financial Checklist asks, "Has the growth rate in earnings been relatively high over the last five years?" If answered "yes," the company is doing well and has exhibited good management practices, particularly if the company is doing better relative to the industry and market. A company with a low rate in earnings growth should be further investigated. A low rate may signal that the company is not managed efficiently, has a large amount of fixed obligations, or is heavily investing in research and development.

Part E requests that earnings per share over the last two years be evaluated to determine if they have been positive. Negative earnings will create negative P/E ratios, which are considered

Figure 3.1. Stock screening and evaluation worksheet

I. Stock History

	19__	19__	19__	19__	19__	19__	Average	Recent
Price:								
High	___	___	___	___	___	___	___	
Low	___	___	___	___	___	___	___	___
Earnings per Share (EPS)	___	___	___	___	___	___	___	___
Dividends per Share (DPS)	___	___	___	___	___	___	___	___
Return on Equity (ROE)	___	___	___	___	___	___	___	
Price-Earnings (P/E):								
High	___	___	___	___	___	___	___	
Low	___	___	___	___	___	___	___	
Ave.	___	___	___	___	___	___	___	
Dividend Yield (Div./Price):								
High	___	___	___	___	___	___	___	
Low	___	___	___	___	___	___	___	
Ave.	___	___	___	___	___	___	___	___

II. Market and Industry Data

	Market	Industry
Price-Earnings (P/E)	___	___
Long-Term Debt-to-Equity		___
Return on Equity (ROE)		___

Continued

Figure 3.1. Stock screening and evalutaion worksheet, *Continued*

III. Financial Checklist

A. Has return on equity (ROE) been high and stable? Yes/No _____

B. Is long-term debt to equity low relative to
industry norms?   Yes/No _____

      Long-term debt _____ / Equity (net worth) _____ = _____

C. Is the current P/E low relative to the
market and industry?   Yes/No _____

D. Has the growth rate in earnings been relatively
high over the last five years?   Yes/No _____

E. Have earnings per share been positive each
year for the last two years?   Yes/No _____

IV. Estimating Range of Value

A. Price-Earnings Method
(For stock considered primarily for capital gains)

Ave. High P/E _____ X Est. Highest Annual EPS _____ = _____ (High)

Ave. Low P/E _____ X Est. Lowest Annual EPS _____ = _____ (Low)

B. Dividend Yield Method
(For stocks considered primarily for dividend yield)

Est. High Annual Div. _____ / Lowest Ave. Div. Yield _____ = _____ (High)

Est. Low Annual Div. _____ / Highest Ave. Div. Yield _____ = _____ (Low)

C. Compare current price _____ to high _____ and low _____ prices.

If current stock price is near or below estimated low price, the stock is a candidate for an investment portfolio. If the security's price is near or above the estimated high price, it should be carefully examined before being added to a portfolio.

Adapted from the *AAII Journal,* September, 1985

meaningless. Using negative P/Es in an analysis will throw off the analysis by lowering the average P/E figure. When negative P/Es are encountered, it is best to discard them from the analysis.

After completing the Financial Checklist section, investors should have a good sense of the company's financial health and management abilities.

Section IV—Estimating Range of Value

Estimating range of value applies the extreme high and low estimates of earnings and dividends to help determine if the stock is currently fairly priced. Completing the valuation process, this section includes both the P/E and dividend yield methods. Again, for stocks being considered primarily for capital gains, Part A should be used; for high paying dividend stocks, Part B should be utilized.

Using the earnings valuation method to determine the estimated highest and lowest price, the average high or low P/E is multiplied by the highest or lowest estimated earnings per share (EPS) for the next year. Using the dividend yield model to calculate the high and low prices, estimated high or low annual dividend is divided by the lowest or highest average dividend yields. When performing either valuation, it is important to remember that as stocks become overpriced dividend yields decrease while P/E ratios increase.

The average, high, and low P/Es and the average, high, and low dividend yields can be gathered from Section I of the worksheet (Figure 3.1).

There are several quick methods investors can use to determine *raw* high and low earnings estimates. First, the earnings history in Section I can be reviewed to get a sense of where earnings will be in the future. A second alternative is to obtain earnings and dividends growth rates from the 5- and 10-year growth rates reported in the *Value Line* one-page company listing under the heading "Annual Rates." When using the *Value Line* rates, however, investors should make sure that the time period selected is representative of the time period being evaluated. *Value Line* estimates for future earnings growth can also be used if investors agree with the reported estimates of future company performance.

Finally, investors wishing to calculate and/or confirm reported earnings *and* dividends estimates can calculate the annually compounded growth rates by applying the following growth rate formula:

$$G_{ern/div} = (E_0/E_1)^{1/n} - 1$$

where:

$G_{ern/div}$ is the historical rate of growth for either
earnings or dividends,
E_0 is the ending year's earnings (dividends) per share,
E_1 is the beginning year's earnings (dividends) per share,
and
n is the number of years compounding.

Note that the number of years compounding is not the same as the number of years being evaluated—the last year does not compound. This formula measures the *rate* at which earnings or dividends increased (compounded), from the first to the last year being evaluated. A range of reasonable prices can now be determined by applying the percent of growth to the last reported earnings or to the latest reported dividends. For example, if:

E_0 = \$3.00
E_1 = \$2.10, and
n = 5

then:

$$G_{ern/div} = (3.00/2.10)^{1/5} - 1$$
$$= .074 \text{ or } 7.4\%.$$

By applying the 7 percent growth rate to the latest earnings reported by *Value Line*, say \$3.10, then a high earnings estimate of \$3.32 can be assumed [3.10 x (1 + .07)]. To determine a lowest price estimate, a lower percentage should be applied. Less conservative investors can increase the percent rate of growth expected.

Part C of this section compares current price to top high and low prices, obtained from the stock history section. If current stock price is near or below the estimated low price, then the intrinsic value of the stock is at parity and should be considered for a portfolio. If the security's price is near or above the estimated high price, it should be carefully examined before being added to a portfolio.

STOCK SCREENING AND EVALUATION EXAMPLE:
Sara Lee Corporation

Data for Sara Lee and the food industry were gathered from the *Value Line Industry Survey* and the market price-earnings ratio, 14.6, was obtained from *S&P's Outlook*. The P/E for the food industry, 13.9, was obtained from *Value Line's Food Industry Composite*, which is reported in the introduction to each specific industry section.

The analysis for Sara Lee Corporation (see Figure 3.2) begins with Section III, the Financial Checklist. From Section I, we learned that Sara Lee has an average return on investment (ROE) of 18.4. However, what stands out is that Sara Lee's ROE declined from 19.4 in 1985 to 18.1 in 1988. This decline indicates that the company's ROE should be closely watched to see if the expected industry ROE of 19 can be matched over the next five years.

Reviewing Sara Lee's long-term debt-to-equity shows that it is slightly below the food industry average (49.6 percent vs. 50.2 percent), but not enough to send out any warning signals. It simply tells us that things are average.

The company's current P/E of 17.1 is high relative to both the market, 14.6, and the food industry P/E, 13.9. This indicates that the market either expects Sara Lee's earnings to grow faster than those of the market or the industry, or that Sara Lee is overvalued by the market.

Examining earnings shows that Sara Lee's growth in earnings has been relatively high over the last five years, indicating that the company is doing well and management practices are sound.

In Section IV, valuing Sara Lee, both the dividend and earnings valuation models have been completed. By applying the growth rate formula over a 5-year period, it was determined that the company's earnings growth rate was 14.5 percent and its dividend growth rate was 15 percent. Half the value of these growth rates was used to determine the low earnings and dividend estimates.

The latest annual earnings reported by *Value Line* was $3.40 and thus an estimated high annual earnings of $3.89 and a low annual earnings of $3.66 were calculated—3.40 x (1 + .145) and 3.40 x (1 + .075). The base of $1.44, the dividend declared for fiscal year 1989, was used to determine dividend estimates.

While current price for Sara Lee is $58 and is within the high ($59.52) and low ($35.06) price range calculated, the price is on the high end of the scale and leaves little room for error should earnings slip below expectations. The dividend yield model shows a

Figure 3.2. Stock screening and evaluation worksheet—Sara Lee Corporation

I. Stock History

	19 83	19 84	19 85	19 86	19 87	19 88	Average	Recent
Price:								
High	13.6	17.4	26.0	36.8	49.1	51.5		
Low	9.5	12.5	15.6	23.6	26.5	32.9		58
Earnings per Share (EPS)	1.44	1.63	1.81	2.02	2.35	2.83	2.01	3.40
Dividends per Share (DPS)	0.57	0.64	0.71	0.78	0.95	1.15	0.80	1.44
Return on Equity (ROE)	18.3	18.3	19.4	18.2	17.9	18.1	18.37	
Price-Earnings (P/E):								
High	9.44	10.67	14.36	18.22	20.89	18.20	15.30	
Low	6.60	7.67	8.62	11.68	11.28	11.63	9.58	
Average	8.02	9.17	11.49	14.95	16.09	14.91	12.44	17.1
Dividend Yield (Div./Price):								
High	4.19	3.68	2.73	2.12	1.93	2.23	2.81	
Low	6.00	5.12	4.55	3.31	3.58	3.50	4.34	
Average	5.10	4.40	3.64	2.71	2.76	2.86	3.58	

II. Market and Industry Data

	Market	Industry
Price-Earnings (P/E)	14.6	13.9
Long-Term Debt-to-Equity		50.2
Return on Equity (ROE)		19.4

III. Financial Checklist

A. Has return on equity (ROE) been high and stable? Yes/No _NO_

B. Is long-term debt to equity low relative to industry norms? Yes/No _NO_

   Long-term debt $893.4 / Equity (net worth) $1,800.1 = _49.6%_

C. Is the current P/E low relative to the market and industry? Yes/No _No_

D. Has the growth rate in earnings been relatively high over the last five years? Yes/No _Yes_

E. Have earnings per share been positive each year for the last two years? Yes/No _Yes_

IV. Estimating Range of Value

A. Price-Earnings Method (For stock considered primarily for capital gains)

   Ave. High P/E _15.3_ X Est. Highest Annual EPS _3.89_ = _59.52_ (High)

   Ave. Low P/E _9.58_ X Est. Lowest Annual EPS _3.66_ = _35.06_ (Low)

B. Dividend Yield Method (For stocks considered primarily for dividend yield)

   Est. High Annual Div. _1.66_ / Lowest Ave. Div. Yield _2.81_ = _59.07_ (High)

   Est. Low Annual Div. _1.55_ / Highest Ave. Div. Yield _4.34_ = _35.71_ (Low)

C. Compare current price $58 to high $59.52 and low $35.06 prices.

similar situation. Had the current price been on the low end of the price estimates, Sara Lee would have represented a better value.

CONCLUSION

When using fundamental analysis to examine companies, investors need to consider many factors. One should first examine whether capital appreciation or income is required. Determining the company and industry's life cycle stages will help to indicate the type of return expected (capital appreciation through aggressive growth and growth companies, and income with more mature companies).

When a potential company or industry has been identified, obtaining and reviewing company annual reports and analyst reports will provide a feel for management's direction and how others expect the company to perform. The annual report will also serve as the source from which to perform ratio analysis to determine the financial strength of the company. Financially-sound companies then need to be examined using techniques such as the stock selection worksheet to determine whether the security is priced fairly. The final decision of adding or deleting a security from an investment portfolio should be based on personal judgement, supported by fundamental analysis. Fundamental analysis requires some work, but the results will be satisfying—financially and emotionally.

Finally, analysts and investors often need to gauge the risk that is common to all securities and cannot be eliminated by diversification, along with the expected returns for taking these risks. *Beta* is a popular measure of security risk that examines how a security, or even a group of securities, performs relative to the market.

Beta

Beta is a relative measure of risk and expected return, with a beta of 1 being equal to the market. Therefore, stocks with returns that rise and fall with the market have a beta of 1. Securities with betas less than 1 tend to be more stable (conservative), moving less than the market moves. Securities with betas greater than 1 tend to be more volatile (aggressive) and risky, moving more than the market. For example, if the market were to go up 10 percent, a security with a beta of .80 would be expected to move 80 percent of what the market moved, or 8 percent. On the other hand, a security with a beta of 1.20 would be expected to move 120 percent of what the market moved, or 12 percent. Of course, if the market were to go down, the security with a high beta would be expected to decrease more than a lower beta security.

Individuals can use beta measurements to select securities or construct a portfolio of securities that is consistent with personal objectives and risk tolerance. For instance, risk takers, or those individuals who can tolerate more risk, would consider securities with betas higher than 1. Conversely, risk averters would select securities with a beta less than 1. Remember, that beta measures the risk inherent to all securities (stock market risk); it does *not* take into account financial or industry risk. In constructing investment portfolios, investors should use beta in conjunction with diversification, the basic principle of diversification being that individuals should invest in those securities with variations of return offsetting one another.

Beta calculations for stocks and mutual funds are widely available. *S&P's Stock Reports* and *Value Line Investment Survey* report on security betas, while publications such as *Morning Star* report on mutual funds.

4 / TECHNICAL ANALYSIS

OVERVIEW

Technical analysis, whether applied to a specific security or to the market as a whole, focuses on the *qualitative* factors of trading. Technicians concentrate on studying chart patterns, price and trading trends, market theories, sentiment indicators, and price action of the market averages and indices to determine what future price and trading patterns will be.

For years fundamental and technical analysts have disagreed regarding the technician's place on Wall Street. Strict fundamentalists cite the Random-Walk Theory as the basis for their case. In a nutshell, the theory states that each successive change in price is statistically independent of the last, that neither the size nor the direction of the last move or set of moves is of any predictive value in determining the size and direction of the next move.

Technical analysts counter this argument in two ways. First, they say "don't fight the tape" and show how their charts have helped them to accurately predict price actions in the past. Second, they point to the number of technical analysts on Wall Street collecting large paychecks. These arguments aside, both technical and fundamental analysts have earned their places on Wall Street. And as long as a sufficient number of investors follow them, the techniques employed will have the characteristics of self-fulfilling prophecies.

SOURCE OF DATA

The primary source of data used in technical analysis is the ticker tape. Originally, the *ticker tape* referred to the data tape that was printed by the old New York Stock Exchange (NYSE) ticker machines. Running at speeds of up to 900 characters per minute, these machines "reported" transactions as they occurred—including ticker symbols, volume, and other specialty characteristics. However, with the onset of the electronic age and the expansion of trading volume, the *ticker tape* has come to refer to the new, faster electronic display boards that have replaced the old ticker machines.

In 1975, a new computerized system was officially implemented to report securities transactions occurring in the various market-places on a single ticker tape system known as the *consolidated tape*. Under this system, all NYSE-listed securities are reported on the NYSE ticker tape (Network A), and all American Stock Exchange (AMEX)-listed and regionally traded securities are reported on the AMEX ticker tape (Network B). The tape now contains more data than it ever did and is also better organized and easier to use.

Identification of the particular exchange on which each transaction occurs is noted by a single letter, as follows:

A - American
B - Boston
C - Cincinnati
M - Midwest
N - New York
O - Instinet (institutional trading system)
P - Pacific
T - Third market (Over-the-Counter—OTC—trading of listed securities)
X - Philadelphia

Figure 4.1 illustrates a sample section of a consolidated ticker tape. It shows the trading activity of Sara Lee Corporation (ticker symbol, SLE), Apple Computer (AAPL), AT&T (T), and Badger Meter (BMI). On the upper line of the reading is the ticker symbol, followed by an ampersand and a letter representing the exchange on which the trade occurred. (Ticker symbols not followed by an exchange designation were traded on the NYSE.) On the lower line, the number that precedes the S indicates a trade in round lots (i.e., 10, 100); the last number represents the price of the trade. Therefore, the first entry indicates that 400 shares of Sara Lee traded at 56 1/2 on the New York Stock Exchange.

Figure 4.1. Consolidated ticker tape sample

SLE	AAPL&T	T&P	BMI&A
4S56 1/2	2S39 5/8	35 3/4	3S18 1/8

Technology aside, the *source* of the data used in technical analysis is still the same—it comes from the tape. Today investors can read the tape at many brokerage firms, watch Financial News Network (FNN), and utilize certain computer services such as Lotus Signal (discussed at the end of this chapter under "Forecasting the Future"). By "reading the tape," technicians are able to discern a number of things about the market: what is being traded, how heavily it is being traded, how fast the market is moving, in what direction it is moving, and how widespread the movement is. By applying a set of time-tested techniques to analyze this data, the technician can "listen" to what the market is saying and invest accordingly.

KEY PIECES OF INFORMATION

The three key pieces of data that technical analysis employs are *price*, *volume*, and the *time* of occurrence. Though used in a variety of ways, several general rules apply to the usage of this information:

- Price movements follow certain patterns (trends) that continue until a change break occurs, at which point they reverse. A change or a break, in the pattern is known as a reversal.

- Trends are identified by examining and following price over time.

- Volume data, when studied in relation to price, is used to confirm or deny the conclusions drawn about trends. Strong volume is generally supportive; weak volume is generally neutral or unsupportive. If strong volume accompanies the formation of a pattern, then the pattern would be expected to continue. Weak volume reduces the predictive confidence of a pattern.

- Momentum, defined as the rate of change in price and volume movement, is used to confirm changes in trends. Increasing momentum supports the continuation of the current trend; decreasing momentum is unsupportive of the direction of the trend and suggests a reversal may follow.

Though these general rules apply to the information used by technicians, analysts tracking the same security may identify different patterns and thus, get different signals.

MANIPULATING DATA

In addition to using price, volume, and time data provided by the tape, technical analysis also employs a number of data-manipulation techniques to glean more information. One such technique is to examine the momentum (the rate of movement) of the data. *Momentum* is calculated by taking the difference between pieces of data separated by a fixed interval of time. For instance, to calculate a five-day momentum value for price, each day's price is subtracted from the price that occurred five days before. Then this new set of data, which represents the "rate of change" in price over a five-day period, is analyzed for its trend. From this, conclusions can be drawn whether a price trend is strengthening or weakening, which in turn will help determine whether the trend is likely to continue or reverse.

Figure 4.2 shows the price for stock X over a two-week period and the resulting five-day momentum calculations. The momentum for the second Monday was computed by subtracting the close of the period five days earlier (21 1/2 on the Monday of week 1) from its close (22 5/8). This process was repeated for the whole week. The momentum calculations for stock X show that while the price of stock X is generally increasing, the rate of change is decreasing —a sign of weakness.

Another frequently used technique examines moving averages of the data. *Moving averages* are used in technical analysis to help smooth out the random day-to-day variations that occur in data, so legitimate trends can be more accurately identified. To calculate moving averages, daily data is summed and divided by the number of days in the selected period. Each successive day, the computation is repeated using the newest day's price and dropping the oldest day's data to keep constant the number of periods used in the moving average.

For instance, a simple three day moving average is constructed by taking a rolling three days' worth of data, summing it, and dividing the resulting number by three. Consider a stock, with closing prices for a week at 30 on Monday, 32 on Tuesday, 31 on Wednesday, 33 on Thursday, and 35 on Friday. The moving average of 31 would be computed on Wednesday by adding 30, 32, and 31 and dividing the result by 3. On Thursday the moving average would be 32—(32 + 31 + 33)/3. Friday's three-day moving average would be 33—(31 + 33 + 35)/3. In this way, the effects of any random occurrence, which would otherwise significantly distort the data, are reduced. By the same token, the effects of any legitimate occurrence are also reduced. Therefore, one should be aware that as the

Figure 4.2. Five-day momentum of stock X

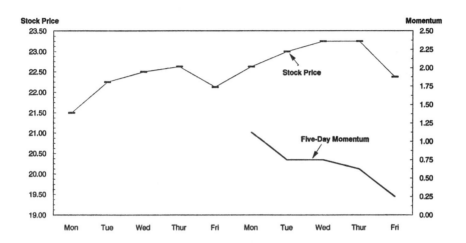

number of days in a moving average increases, the indicator becomes less responsive to short-term fluctuations and is slower to identify changes in trends.

A number of other variations are used to determine the moving average. The moving average just presented is a *simple moving average* because is treats all data used in the computation equally, ignoring whether the data is new or old. In contrast, *weighted moving averages* apply weighing factors to some of the data, typically giving the most recent data the heaviest weighing in order to give it added importance.

Some technical systems go so far as to ignore current data in favor of moving average data; others study the relationship between current data and moving average data or between sets of moving average data. However, all technical systems that employ moving averages generally follow the same set of basic rules: buy when prices move above the moving average and sell when prices move below the moving average.

A number of other proprietary techniques have been developed using data manipulated in a variety of fashions. Just about every well-known technician has developed some methodology to draw conclusions about the market. And because each of these technical gurus uses slightly different methodology, it should be no surprise to find them making public pronouncements at different times with different objectives in mind—all from reading the same "tape."

Technical analysis provides investors a set of tools to use when making investment decisions. Some investors will use technical analysis exclusively in selecting securities. Others will select likely candidates with fundamental analysis and use technical analysis to help determine entry and exit points for securities. Even those investors using fundamental analysis exclusively should examine the following discussion of technical analysis to understand what trends are driving technicians.

CHARTS AND TRENDS

Charts are used by market technicians to describe and evaluate the price actions occurring in the market. Charts are helpful in identifying trends; spotting changes in trends, known as *reversals*; underscoring significant trading developments; and predicting the timing and strength of future developments. Several different charting methods are used, but the two most predominant are point and figure charts, and vertical line (or bar) charts.

Using a series of Xs to represent price rises and a series of Os to represent price declines, point and figure charts plot price movements without regard to the timing of such movements. These charts reflect significant price changes and the direction of those changes (see Figure 4.3).

Vertical line charts plot price movements through a series of vertical lines. In these charts, the vertical axis represents price and volume, and the horizontal axis represents time. Variations of line charts include close-only charts; high, low charts; open, high, low charts; and open, high, low, close charts. Often the volume will be plotted along the bottom of the chart. For example an open, high, low, close chart uses vertical lines to represent the extent of the price move, with the ends of each line representing the high and low price and the horizontal bars on the left and right side of each line representing the opening and closing prices, respectively (see Figure 4.4). Close-only charts plot the closing prices only (see Figure 4.5).

Figure 4.3.   **Figure 4.4.**   **Figure 4.5.**

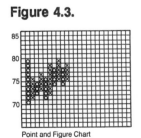

Point and Figure Chart

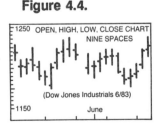

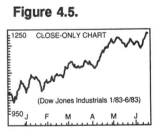

Trendlines are helpful in determining the current market trends by identifying the overall direction of the market. Trendlines help technicians decide whether to have long or short positions in the market. Very brief trends are *minor trends*; those lasting a few weeks are *intermediate trends*; and those lasting for a period of months are *major trends*.

In an up market, the trendline is drawn by connecting each successively higher "bottom," as illustrated in Figure 4.6. As long as the market remains on or above the line, the *uptrend* remains in force.

In a down market, the trendline is drawn by connecting each successively lower "top" (see Figure 4.7). As long as the market remains on or below this line, the *downtrend* remains in force.

Figure 4.6.

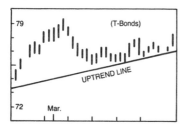

Figure 4.7.

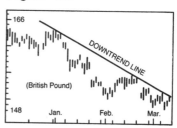

The theory behind trendlines is that when a trendline is penetrated, the trend will reverse. Thus if an uptrend line is penetrated, a downtrend is put in force and, from a technical basis, it is time to sell. Conversely, if a downtrend line is penetrated, an uptrend is put in force and it is time to buy.

The slope of a trendline is also very important. The steeper the trendline the more easily it can be broken. Even a brief sideward movement can break the trend. Thus, extremely steep trendlines are not considered very authoritative, whereas gentler sloping trendlines are.

Other factors to consider in evaluating trendlines are the number of tops or bottoms that have formed to support the trendline and the duration of the trendline. A large number of tops and bottoms over a long period of time help to validate the existence of a trend, its magnitude, and the effort that will be required to reverse the trend.

As trendlines are penetrated new trendlines are drawn, creating a pattern of *fan lines* (see Figure 4.8). Though trendline theory suggests that a reversal occurs when a trendline is penetrated, the penetration must be analyzed to determine its relative validity. This is done by examining what the volume was at the time of occurrence and what the closing price of the security was for the day. The rule of thumb is that when the third fan line is broken, the trend has indeed been reversed.

Usually, when a trendline has been legitimately penetrated, a *pullback* will occur. That is, when an uptrend is broken, a security will sell off for a few days and then rally back before it begins to finally trend lower (see Figure 4.9).

Figure 4.8.   **Figure 4.9.**

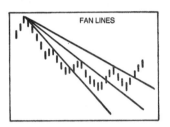
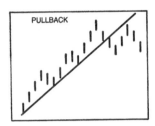

During the normal course of trading, price levels will be reached that temporarily halt a downward movement in price; these are *support levels*. By the same token, price levels will be reached that temporarily halt an upward movement in price. Such points are called *resistance levels* (see Figures 4.10 and 4.11).

Figure 4.10.   **Figure 4.11.**

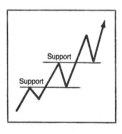
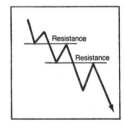

Support and resistance levels occur for many reasons, including a concentration of demand (support), a concentration of supply (resistance), former tops, and former bottoms. A downtrend (a former bottom), once penetrated, becomes a resistance level. Once surpassed, an uptrend (a former top) becomes a support level. A congestion area, once broken out of, becomes either a support or a resistance level depending on the direction of the trend.

Note that once a support or resistance level has been tested, it is weakened. Tested again, it may still hold. Tested a third time, however, it will usually give way. When taking a position in a security, investors should examine previous tops or bottoms to determine potential support or resistance levels through which the security will have to pass.

REVERSAL PATTERNS

Reversal patterns predict future price movements by identifying trend changes as they occur. Though price action itself is the primary means used to identify these trend changes, more often than not timing and volume validation is required to confirm such conclusions.

Major Reversals

To reverse intermediate or major up or down trends, significant price and volume action must occur. Typically, these patterns will take on one of the following formations.

Head and Shoulders Tops signify an upcoming decline. In this pattern, one of the most reliable of all reversal patterns, the "left shoulder" is usually formed at the end of an extensive, high volume advance. The "head" then forms on heavy upside volume and lighter downside volume, and the "right shoulder" forms on a rally with less volume than either of the two previous rallies. As illustrated in Figure 4.12, penetration or breakout of the "neckline" (the line formed by the bottoms of the two shoulders), provides final confirmation of the reversal and completes the pattern. Be aware that most head and shoulders patterns are not perfectly symmetrical and will require attentive examination to identify.

Head and Shoulders Bottoms signify an upcoming rally. Though the chart pattern appears to be an inverted head and shoulders top, the volume pattern is different (see Figure 4.13). Here, volume in-

Figures 4.12.

Figure 4.13.

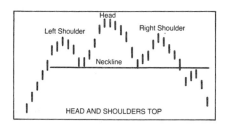

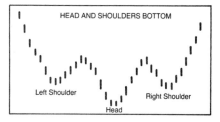

creases as the price rallies from the bottom of the head and increases even more dramatically on the rally from the right shoulder. The major factor to watch in the head and shoulders bottom formation is the activity on the right shoulder. If a dramatic increase in volume on the rally from the right shoulder does not occur, it may signify a false bottom and the downtrend will most likely continue.

Double Top formations indicate an upcoming decline. Probably one of the trickiest patterns to identify, a double top forms after a significant rally. True double tops are differentiated from consolidation patterns (discussed later) through validation of volume, time, and extent of decline from the highs. For a true double top to occur, the first sell-off should be deep and long, as investors take profits. The right top should occur on lighter volume than the left top, indicating decreasing uptrend strength. Finally, the lows separating the left and right tops should be easily broken by the sell·off from the right top, indicating the start of the downtrend (see Figure 4.14). Correctly identifying this formation will allow conservative investors to sell their holdings; more aggressive investors can take short positions to attempt a profit on downward price movement.

Double Bottoms signify an upcoming rally. Though the chart pattern appears to be an upside-down image of the double top, the volume pattern is different—the volume on the rally from the second bottom will show a great increase over the volume on the first rally, indicating strong buying pressure for the upcoming rally (as shown in Figure 4.15). This pattern indicates that it is time to unwind any short positions and go long.

Figure 4.14.   **Figure 4.15.**

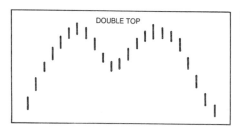

Triple Tops signify an upcoming decline. A triple top shows that a security has tried to penetrate some price level but failed. The triple top typically forms after a long advance and is comprised of a sell-off, a light volume rally, another sell-off, a still lighter volume rally, and another sell-off, the last one penetrating both valleys. As the market rallies, the decreasing volume indicates the decrease in buying demand, allowing selling pressure to gain momentum. *Triple Bottoms* indicate an upcoming rally. Though the chart pattern appears to be an upside-down image of the triple top, the volume pattern differs. The volume on the rallies grows after each bottom, indicating growing buying pressure for the rally off the third bottom. Triple tops and bottoms are illustrated in Figures 4.16 and 4.17.

Figure 4.16. **Figure 4.17.**

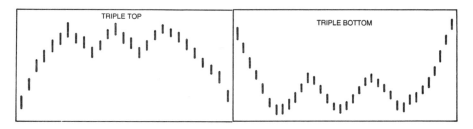

Minor Reversals

Some price action, though not strong enough to reverse intermediate or major trends, is strong enough to reverse minor trends. These patterns will take on one of the following configurations.

Rising Wedges, which signify an upcoming decline, are characteristically denoted by an upper boundary line, constructed from successive tops, slanting up at an angle more shallow than the lower boundary line, constructed from successive bottoms. This rising wedge-shaped pattern suggests a price decline will occur as soon as the lower boundary line is penetrated. Note that rising wedges are applicable only in bear markets—otherwise they represent "flags" or "pennants."

Falling Wedges signify an upcoming rally. Price action moving out of a falling wedge is quite different from that of the rising wedge. Typically, the price is apt to drift sideways and "saucer-out" before it begins to rise. Rising and falling wedges are illustrated in Figures 4.18 and 4.19.

Reversal Day Tops signify an upcoming decline. This trading pattern occurs when prices move higher throughout the day but then close near the lows of the day. Typically, the close is below both the opening and the midpoint of the day's range (see Figure 4.20). *Reversal Day Bottoms*, which indicate an upcoming rally, occur when prices move lower throughout the day but close near the

Figures 4.18.

Figure 4.19.

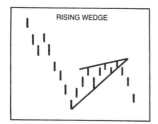

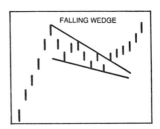

highs of the day. Typically, the close is above both the opening and the midpoint of the day's range, as shown in Figure 4.21.

Figure 4.20.

Figure 4.21.

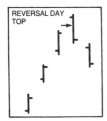

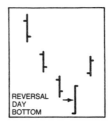

Reversal patterns are used by technical analysts to identify trend changes as they occur, which allows the analysts to adapt the proper strategy for a rally or a decline as it is starting rather than after it is well under way. When examining reversal patterns it is important to carefully study the volume that accompanies the price movements to avoid false signals.

CONSOLIDATION PATTERNS

Markets do not always move up or down. Sometimes a market will move sideways as market participants reevaluate the market. These movements can be extremely brief or last a considerable length of time. In fact, these sideways movements can even penetrate a trend before the market resumes its previous course. Therefore, it is imperative to be able to recognize these sideways movements for what they are, so that such "consolidation" patterns will not be confused with true reversals that will indicate a rally or a decline.

Triangles

Triangles describe a sideways movement in price action resulting from the indecisiveness by both buyers and sellers. Triangles represent a period of consolidation from which prices will almost always continue in the direction of the original trend. Typically, they are characterized by a narrowing in the range of trading highs and lows accompanied by *decreasing* volume. Then when breakout does occur, it is usually accompanied by a sharp *increase* in volume.

The Symmetrical Triangle (Figure 4.22) is formed by a succession of narrowing price fluctuations, resulting in a chart pattern bound by both a downslanting line and an upslanting line. Each symmetrical triangle, by definition, must have at least four reversal points.

Normally, breakout from a symmetrical triangle results in a continuation of the trend, although from time to time reversals have been known to occur. If volume is light when a breakout occurs in the same direction as the trend, it may be a false move called an *end run*, and the trend may soon be penetrated. On the other hand, if volume is heavy and the breakout occurs in the opposite direction of the trend, then it may be a false move called a *shake out*. The trend then may continue along its original course. Figures 4.23 and 4.24 illustrate the end run and shake out.

Figure 4.22.   **Figure 4.23.**   **Figure 4.24.**

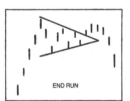

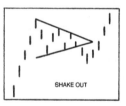

Ascending Right Angles are formed by a succession of narrowing price fluctuations, resulting in a chart pattern bound by an upsloping line and a horizontal line (see Figure 4.25). As the triangle lengthens, trading volume tends to diminish. Typically, when prices finally break, they will break out on the upside. This formation occurs when a large number of sellers ask the same price for securities.

Descending Right Angles, created by a succession of narrowing price fluctuations, result in a chart pattern bound by a downsloping line and a horizontal line (see Figure 4.26). As the triangle lengthens, volume tends to diminish; when prices finally break, they usually break out on the downside. This formation occurs when there is a large demand to buy securities at a fixed price.

Figure 4.25.

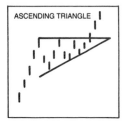

Figure 4.26.

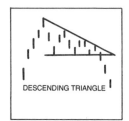

Rectangles

Rectangles are formed as a result of a battle between two groups (buyers and sellers) at different fixed prices. The pattern forms as buying pressure exists at a lower fixed price, not allowing prices to drop further, and selling pressure exists at a higher fixed price, not allowing the prices to rise above the fixed price. This pattern, illustrated in Figure 4.27, appears on a chart as a sideways movement bound by a horizontal line on both the top and bottom. As the rectangle lengthens, volume tends to diminish as the buy and sell orders are satisfied. Breakouts, when they finally do occur, are likely to be followed by a pullback.

Figure 4.27

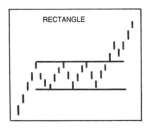

Flags and Pennants

Flags and *Pennants* occur after a dynamic, nearly straight move up or down, that occurs on heavy volume. On the chart a pennant looks similar to a flag, except that the pennant is bound by converging rather than parallel lines. Both flags and pennants are quite reliable indicators that the trend will continue, though they must conform to three rules in order to be valid: first, they should occur after a very sharp move up or down; second, volume should decline as the pattern lengthens; and third, prices must break out of the pattern within a few weeks. Flags and pennants are depicted in Figures 4.28 and 4.29, respectively.

The ability to recognize and identify consolidation patterns is an important aspect of technical analysis. Technicians can avoid the costly error of reversing a position before the rally or decline finishes running its course.

Figure 4.28.

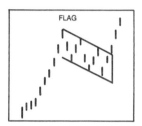

Figure 4.29.

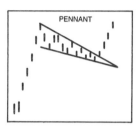

GAPS

When a market is rapidly trading, sometimes *gaps*, or holes, occur in the trading pattern. A gap is formed in an up market when the highest price one day is lower than the lowest price the following day, or in a down market when the lowest price one day is higher than the highest price the following day. Gaps occur with excessive buying or selling pressure, causing prices to jump in order to fill the orders. Though most gaps mark the beginning or end of a trend, some are found in the middle. Therefore it is imperative to be able to determine which type of gap has occurred to avoid getting on the wrong side of a market.

Common Gaps are formed when order imbalances occur during sideways trading ranges known as congestion areas. In this kind of trading pattern, once a gap has occurred prices move up and down through the trading range until they eventually return to the price level of the gap (see Figure 4.30). Then they trade normally through the gap area, thereby acting to "fill the gap."

Figure 4.30.

Figure 4.31.

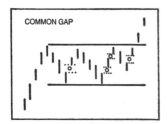

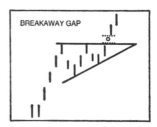

Common gaps, which are a relatively frequent occurrence in consolidation patterns, are a signal that a breakout is going to occur and that the breakout will be in the same direction as the preceding trend. Common gaps are also called by a number of other names, including congestion gaps, temporary gaps, pattern gaps, and area gaps.

Breakaway Gaps occur as prices break away from areas of congestion, especially from those patterns known as *ascending* or *descending triangles*. The significance of a breakaway gap (see Figure 4.31) is that it demonstrates the strength behind the "change in sentiment" (see "Sentiment Theories," discussed later in this chapter) that caused the gap in the first place.

If a breakaway gap occurs during extremely heavy volume, the market most likely will not fill the gap, and prices will continue to move in the direction of the trend. However, if volume is relatively light on a breakaway gap, there is a good chance the gap will be filled before prices resume their trend.

Measuring Gaps are formed during rapid, straightline advances or declines, usually at the midpoint of a move. Because they occur at the halfway point, they are enormously helpful for approximating the move's ultimate price objective. To do this, double the distance between the beginning point and the measuring gap. Figure 4.32 depicts a measuring gap.

Exhaustion Gaps occur at the end of a large, rapid move and signal the end of the move (see Figure 4.33). Unfortunately, a major problem with exhaustion gaps is that they can easily be mistaken for measuring gaps. A mistake of this nature could be very costly, so it is imperative to confirm an exhaustion gap before drawing any conclusions. To do this, keep in mind these two important facts: typically, exhaustion gaps are accompanied by particularly heavy volume; and exhaustion gaps have been known to occur in conjunction with reversal day patterns.

Figure 4.32.

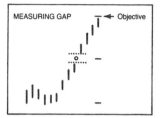

Figure 4.33.

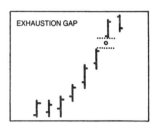

Island Gaps or *Island Reversals* are formed when an exhaustion gap is followed very closely by another gap at or around the same price point but occurring in the opposite direction of the previous trend. This kind of price action isolates the trading that occurs between the two gaps, creating an "island of activity" that is separated from the rest of the trading pattern.

Though a rare occurrence, an island gap is an extremely good indicator of a trend reversal, graphically demonstrating the strength behind the change in sentiment. Figure 4.34 illustrates an island gap.

Figure 4.34

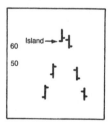

MARKET THEORIES

Though some technical analysis theories have worked well for brief periods of time and then failed, several theories have lasted long enough to be well respected and are used throughout the technical community to predict the future movement of the market.

Dow Theory

The Dow theory is based on the writings of Charles Dow, an editor of *The Wall Street Journal* in the early 1900s. His theory proposes that market averages rise or fall in advance of similar changes in business activity, because investors price securities based on expected future business profitability. Therefore, by properly reading the Dow Jones averages, one can predict future market trends.

According to the Dow theory, there are three basic market movements:

> • *Primary Movement (Major Trend)*—a long-term trend lasting from one to five years, typically known as a bull market for an uptrend or a bear market for a downtrend.

> • *Secondary Movement (Intermediate Trend)*—a reverse of the primary movement, lasting for a short period of time, typically from one to three months. Many such shifts will occur during a bull or bear market before there is a reversal in the primary trend. Secondary movements provide information for medium-term trading decisions, and they help identify the life expectancy of the primary movement. In this regard, the theory states that a major trend is reversed only when it is penetrated by a secondary movement.

> • *Day-to-Day Movement (Minor Trend)*—a series of fluctuations, usually lasting fewer than six days, that are of little consequence. (Collectively, however, they could comprise a secondary movement.)

Advance-Decline Theory

The advance-decline theory is based on the breadth-of-the-market index. This index is computed by taking the net advance-decline figure for an exchange and dividing it by the total number of issues traded on the exchange that day. Examined against previous figures, an indication of whether the market as a whole is gaining or losing strength is given.

If the advance-decline net balance is cumulatively positive, the market may have enough strength to reach for higher ground. Conversely, if net declines continually surpass net advances, the market may be facing a sell-off.

Short Interest "Cushion" Theory

The short interest "cushion" theory states that at some point short sellers will become buyers of stock to cover their positions, and the trading cushion of these potential buyers will either support a declining market or accelerate a rising one. Short interest is calculated by dividing the total number of short sales outstanding on the NYSE by the average daily trading volume on the exchange for the month. The "NYSE Short-Interest Ratio" is published monthly in *Barron's* (see Figure 4.35).

Short interest above one day's average trade volume is bullish and short interest one-and-one-half times greater than daily volume indicates a "buy" signal.

Figure 4.35. Barron's NYSE short-interest ratio

NYSE SHORT-INTEREST RATIO

The short interest ratio is the number of trading days at average volume required to cover the total short interest.

The short interest is the number of shares that have not been purchased, but eventually must be, for return to the lenders.

Year to Date
1989

Jan.	3.75	Apr.	3.54
Feb.	2.97	May	3.27
Mar.	3.22	June	3.03

1988

Jan.	2.10	July	2.41
Feb.	2.18	Aug.	2.77
Mar.	2.34	Sept.	3.16
Apr.	2.60	Oct.	3.12
May	2.91	Nov.	3.16
June	3.13	Dec.	3.84

1987

Jan.	2.78	July	2.82
Feb.	2.22	Aug.	2.96
Mar.	2.61	Sept.	2.59
Apr.	2.58	Oct.	2.90
May	2.37	Nov.	1.62
June	2.89	Dec.	2.85

Source: Reprinted by permission of *Barron's*. ©Dow Jones & Company, Inc., 1989. All rights reserved worldwide.

Confidence Theory

The confidence theory states that price movements are based on increases and decreases in the amount of confidence investors hold regarding the future trends of the market. Simply stated, the feelings investors have regarding what the *future* holds are said to be more important than the feelings they hold about the *present*.

Barron's calculates and publishes a weekly confidence index that uses bond yields to measure investors' willingness to assume risk. This index is based on the presumption that when the yield differential between high-grade bonds and low-grade bonds contracts, investors have greater confidence, are willing to assume more risk, and thus expect the market to rise. By the same reasoning, when the yield differential expands, the market is expected to fall.

Dow Jones Utility Average Theory

The Dow Jones Utility Average theory states that the Dow Jones Utility Average is a leading indicator of changing trends in the stock market. The basis for this assumption is simple: because utility stocks are so interest-sensitive, they tend to react more quickly to changes in the expectation for interest rates. Thus, if the Dow Jones Utility Average is moving up, expectations are that interest rates will fall. Lower interest rates, of course, mean that the cost of doing business will be lowered, that corporate profitability will rise, and that the market is sure to follow.

If the current reading for the Dow Jones Utility Average plots *above* its own fifteen-week moving average, then the market as a whole can be considered to be in an uptrend. By the same token, when the current reading drops *below* its fifteen-week moving average, the market as a whole can be considered in a downtrend.

Retracement Theory

Technicians have noted that markets never seem to move steadily in one direction or the other but "seesaw" toward their eventual price objectives. With this in mind, retracement theory suggests that each movement in the primary direction of the trend is followed by some reaction or retracement in the opposite direction, and that the amount of retracement is some mathematical function of the primary move.

Though typical retracements recapture from one-third to two-thirds of the primary move, most technicians agree that 50 percent of the move is the single most likely amount of retracement to expect. Several noted technicians have done considerable work based on the assumptions of the retracement theory. Some have applied Fibonnaci numbers to this theory. (Fibonnaci was a mathematician born in 1170, who noted uniqueness in number sequences based on his study of the breeding rates of rabbits.) Many technicians use his mathematical concept to analyze price movements. The Gann and Elliott Wave Theories are also based on the general concept of retracement theory.

These market theories have large followings that act and influence the market. Some, such as the Dow Jones Utility Average, tie economic factors to movements. Others, such as the Confidence Theory, attempt to read the minds of market participants. All in all, it is important for both technicians and fundamentalists to understand the effects of these theories so they can be applied and the actions of their followers understood.

SENTIMENT THEORIES

Odd-Lot Purchases and Short Sales Theory

Based on the fact that the "odd-lot" customer frequently does the right thing at the wrong time, this theory suggests that a trend toward increased odd-lot selling is bullish, whereas a trend toward decreased odd-lot selling is bearish.

The odd-lot short sale ratio is calculated by dividing the odd-lot short sales on the NYSE by the weekly total short sales of all NYSE participants. The odd-lot purchase ratio is calculated by dividing total odd-lot purchases on the NYSE by the weekly total purchases of all NYSE participants. Both sets of figures can be found in *Barron's* and *The Wall Street Journal*, although there is a two-week lag in the publication of this data, giving time for the NYSE to collect the information from the firms that trade on the exchange. The higher the odd-lot short sale ratio and the lower the odd-lot purchase ratio, the more bearish the small investor—thus the more bullish the market.

Specialist Short Sales Theory

The specialist short sales theory is based on the principle that the "smart money" knows what is about to happen in the market. Thus, the theory suggests that heavy specialist short selling is bearish, and light specialist short selling is bullish.

The specialist short sales ratio is computed by dividing the weekly total of shares sold short by the NYSE specialists by the weekly total of shares sold short by all NYSE participants. These figures are available in *Barron's* and *The Wall Street Journal*, though there is a two-week lag in the publication or this data.

When a one-week reading falls below 33 percent, or the average of the past four weekly readings is below 35 percent, a buy signal is generated. A sell signal is generated when a one-week reading exceeds 58 percent or the average of the past four weekly readings exceeds 55 percent.

Member Short Sales Theory

Similar to the specialist short sales theory, the member short sales theory suggests that heavy short selling on the part of the members is bearish, and light short selling on the part of members is bullish.

The member short sales ratio is calculated by dividing the weekly total number of shares sold short by members of the NYSE by the weekly total number of shares sold short by all NYSE participants. This data, published two weeks after it is reported, is available in *Barron's* and *The Wall Street Journal*.

Member short sales ratio readings under 65 percent suggest that members are extremely bullish, oftentimes indicating that a major or intermediate market uptrend may be at hand.

Member Trading Theory

The member trading theory suggests that net buying by members is a bullish sign, whereas net selling by members is a bearish sign. Net buying or selling is calculated by subtracting the number of shares sold by NYSE members from the number of shares bought by NYSE members. This data is available in *Barron's* and *The Wall Street Journal* two weeks after it is reported.

Note that some technicians feel that an exponential moving average of member net buying is one of the best indicators of changes in intermediate and major trends.

Advisory Sentiment Theory

The advisory sentiment theory takes a contrarian look at the opinions held by investment advisors. The theory suggests that as a group, investment advisors are slow to recognize the beginning of a bull market, though they typically turn bullish very quickly after market prices have started up. By the same token, they are very poor in picking the top of a bull market, which is the start of a bear market. However, when this group turns overly pessimistic, with 60 percent or more expressing negative sentiments, it usually means that the bear market has just bottomed out.

An excellent source for reading on advisory sentiment is the "Sentiment Index of Advisory Services," maintained by *Chartcraft Investors Intelligence.*

Customer's Margin Debt Theory

The customer's margin debt theory suggests that the buying patterns of margin investors are a good indicator of the future trend of the market. That is, when these sophisticated investors are borrowing money heavily to buy into the market, the future market trend will be up. By the same standard, when these individuals are liquidating stocks and reducing their margin debt, it is a good indicator that the market will be moving lower. On the last trading day of each month, the NYSE calculates the total amount of debt owed to member firms by their customers. The information is not released for two to three weeks, after which it is available directly from the NYSE and also published in *Barron's.*

In analyzing a plot of customer margin debt against its own twelve-month moving average, buy signals are generated whenever the current figure moves above the moving average line, and sell signals are generated whenever the figure moves below it.

Free Credit Balance Theory

The free credit balance theory is based on the fact that only small, less-sophisticated investors allow money to sit idly in a free credit balance with a brokerage firm. Thus, the theory suggests that when this free credit balance increases it is a sign that small, less-sophisticated investors have decided to raise cash, which in turn is a sign that the market will be moving higher. On the other hand, when this balance falls it is a sign that the market will be moving lower. Total free credit balance held by member firms is calculated monthly by the NYSE and is available directly from the exchange. It is also published in *Barron's.*

AAII Individual Investor Sentiment Survey

Though the Individual Investor Sentiment Survey is not a theory, it is worth noting. The American Association of Individual Investors polls its members daily and reports the bullish, bearish, and neutral sentiment weekly. With Individual Investors Sentiment a contrarian indicator, a sustained bullish percentage above 45 percent, is considered indicative of a market decline. A sustained bullish percentage below 20 percent is indicative of a market upswing.

Because the sentiment readings can be volatile, a moving average is often constructed to provide an indication of the overall trend. The results of the AAII Individual Investors Sentiment Survey are published in the Association's monthly *AAII Journal* (see Figure 4.36), and *Barron's*.

Figure 4.36. AAII Individual Investor Sentiment Survey

Source: Reprinted with permission, *AAII Journal*, July 1989.

In an effort to determine the future direction of the market, sentiment theories attempt to measure the moods of the market by examining the feelings of the market's key participants. These theories, in addition to being interesting to follow, are helpful in market forecasting as well as illuminating what other market players are doing.

BREADTH-OF-MARKET and SHORT-TERM TRADING INDICATORS

Breadth-of-market indicators are used to measure how widespread market trading patterns have become. In addition to acting as a barometer of the market's general condition, they also help determine what phase of the trend the market is in and the length of time left in the phase. Short-term indicators also measure the market's condition, looking at internal activity on a moment-to-moment basis.

The Advance-Decline Line

The advance-decline line is the most commonly used indicator for measuring the condition of the market. It is calculated by taking the difference between the number of advancing and the number of declining issues on a daily basis, and adding or subtracting the resulting number to a running total. The running total is then plotted over time, and the resulting chart is used to draw conclusions about the internal strength or weakness of the market. *Investor's Daily* charts the DJIA advance-decline line in the general market indicators section, as shown in Figure 4.37.

In general, when the advance-decline line is rising, the market is gathering internal strength, and higher prices are in store. Conversely, when the advance-decline line is falling, the market is losing strength and lower prices will follow. At market tops and bottoms, the advance-decline line diverges from the trend of the market averages, showing weakness before the market hits the top and strength before the market hits the bottom. Experience has shown that the advance-decline line is better at picking tops than at picking bottoms.

Many proprietary indicators and indices have been developed that use the advance-decline line as a basis for analysis. Some of these methodologies employ moving averages of the advance-decline line, others analyze the relationship of the advance-decline line to its moving average, and still others apply weights to the advance-decline line based on time or trading volume.

The Unchanged Issues Index

The unchanged issues index is a commonly used indicator for measuring the condition of the market. It is calculated by dividing the number of issues that remain unchanged in price each day by the total number of stocks traded during the day. The number of unchanged issues and volume information can be found in *The Wall Street Journal*. In general, this index ranges from 5 to 25 percent. Readings close to 5 percent are considered bullish; readings close to 25 percent are considered bearish.

Figure 4.37. DIJA Advance-Decline Line, *Investor's Daily*

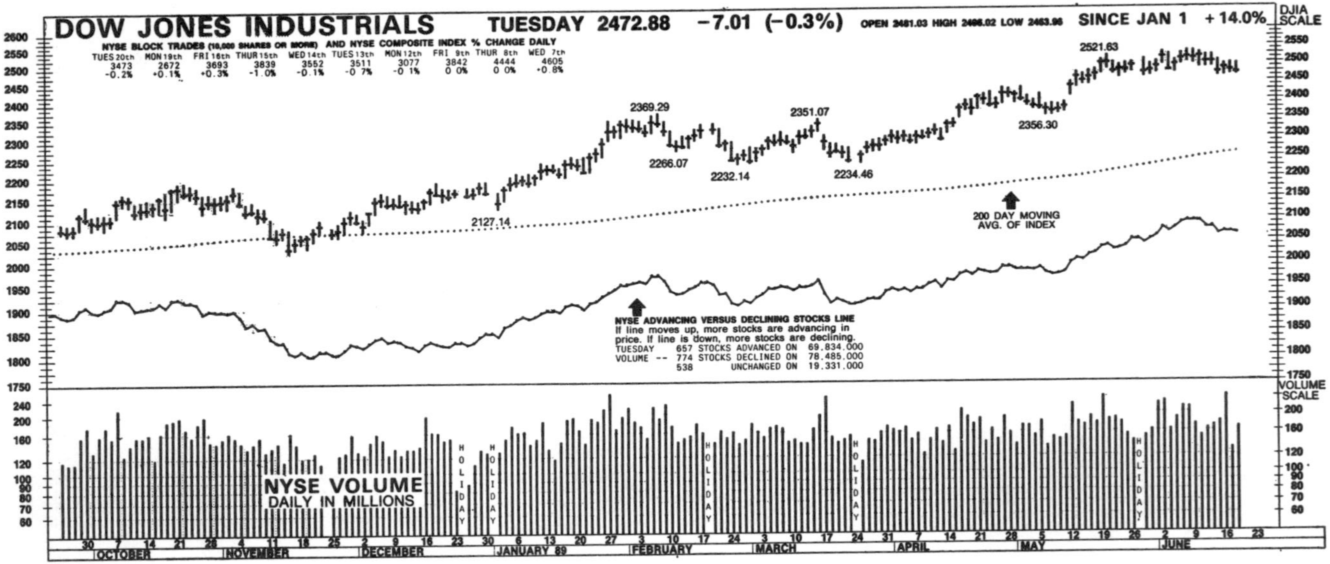

Source: Reprinted by permission of *Investor's Daily*, America's Business Newspaper, June 21, 1989. © Investor's Daily, Inc. 1989.

Relative Strength

Relative strength is a measure of an industry group's market performance compared with the market's overall performance. It is calculated by comparing the performance of each industry group against the performance of the New York Stock Exchange Composite Index, and then rank ordering each industry group in terms of its relative strength to all the other groups. *Investor's Daily* selects a different industry each day and plots its relative strength against the S&P 500. *Investor's Daily* also maintains index values on 200 industry groups for investors wishing to plot relative strength. In general, it is better to buy issues in strong industry groups than weak ones since the strong industry groups, by their very definition, are leading the market.

The Most Active Issues

The most active issues represent those stocks that are trading the most volume each day. A list of the most active issues for the NYSE, AMEX, and NASDAQ National Market system is published daily in *Investor's Daily* and *The Wall Street Journal*.

The most active issues list is used in two ways: to determine what "class" of stocks is leading the market, and to determine what direction the market will move in the near term. In order to determine the class of leadership, each issue on the list is cross-referenced against its price. Then the percentage of issues priced at or above the arbitrary price of $40 per share is calculated. When this percentage exceeds 50 percent, the market is said to be led by *quality* issues. When this percentage is below 50 percent, the market is said to be led by *speculative* issues. Quality markets show internal strength; speculative markets show internal weakness.

When used for determining the near-term direction of the market, each issue on the list is examined to see if it shows a gain for the day. Then a "percentage gainer" figure is calculated and worked into a ten-day moving average from which a chart is constructed. The chart is then analyzed according to the following rules: (1) a chart showing the indicator moving into the 60 to 70 percent region and turning down predicts a short-term correction; (2) a chart showing the indicator moving into the 60 to 70 percent region and continuing up predicts a powerful near-term rally; (3) a chart showing the indicator moving into the 30 to 35 percent region and turning up predicts a short-term rally; and (4) a chart showing the indicator moving into the 30 to 35 percent region and continuing down predicts a further near-term decline.

New Highs and Lows List

The new highs and lows list represents stocks that are at new highs or new lows for the past fifty-two-week period. This list is published daily in *Investor's Daily* and *The Wall Street Journal*.

Generally speaking, when the number of new highs is expanding, it is a bullish sign for the market, especially if the number of new lows is contracting. Conversely, if the number of new highs is contracting while the number of new lows is expanding, it is a bearish sign for the market. As with most indicators, it is imperative to consider what phase the market is in and what types of divergences are occurring between these indicators and the market before any intelligent conclusions can be drawn.

Short-Term Trading Index (TRIN) or Arms Index

TRIN evaluates buying and selling pressure in the market by measuring the amount of volume going into advancing issues versus the amount of volume going into declining issues. It is calculated as follows:

$$\text{TRIN} = \frac{(\text{\# of advancing issues}/\text{\# of declining issues})}{(\text{upside volume}/\text{downside volume})}$$

For instance, if the number of advancing issues is greater than the number of declining issues, the numerator of the equation will be greater than one. In addition, if the volume of these advancing issues is greater than the volume of declining issues, the denominator will also be greater than one. If the relative ratio of advances to declines is less than the relative ratio of advancing to declining volume, the numerator will be smaller than the denominator and the equation will generate a reading between 0 and 1. The reading then suggests that the market is bullish—the lower the number the more bullish.

TRIN readings can be interpreted as follows: below .65, very bullish; .65 to .90, bullish; .90 to 1.10, neutral; and above 1.10, bearish. TRIN is continuously calculated throughout the trading day, and its readings reflect extremely short-term market sentiment. The closing TRIN is published daily in *The Wall Street Journal*.

Cumulative Tick

Cumulative tick is the single most sensitive of all market indicators. It is calculated by subtracting the total number of stocks that have traded down in price from their previous trade (known as "down-ticks") from the total number of stocks that have traded up in price from their previous trade (known as "upticks"). Readings above +100 are considered bullish; readings from -100 to +100 are considered neutral; and readings below -100 are considered bearish. The tick is continuously calculated throughout the trading day, and the closing tick is published daily in *The Wall Street Journal*.

Breadth-of-market theories try to gauge the force behind market moves and are helpful in judging whether the market has the strength to continue a trend or is headed for a reversal.

FORECASTING THE FUTURE

Technical analysis relies on the manipulation and interpretation of great quantities of price and volume data. Because computers make it possible to apply analytical techniques that would be nearly impossible to do otherwise, they are playing a greater role in technical analysis. With the computer, an analyst can quickly and easily plot price and volume information across a number of securities and market indices, then compute and test the effectiveness of various techniques on a variety of different securities. Computers also permit both analysts and investors greater individual choice as to which securities to follow and which techniques to apply. Thus, investors no longer need to rely on chart services and can perform propriety analysis on a semi-instantaneous basis.

With a computer and a link to an on-line data service, investors can study market movement throughout the day and participate in the market on a shorter-term basis. Individuals can retrieve information quickly, automatically, and relatively inexpensively. With an electronic quote service such as Lotus Signal, investors can receive real-time quotes on personal computers, using either a special FM-based receiver or a satellite hookup. Telemet provides a similar service but offers the option of real-time quotes or less expensive, fifteen-minute delayed quotes. Other services, such as Data Broadcasting Corporation, provide connections to the exchanges through regular cable TV linkups. Channels such as FNN also broadcast special signals that most personal computers can read.

For investors with PC data services such as CompuServe, Dow Jones News/Retrieval, and Warner Computer Systems, historical price and volume information is only a phone call away. These services provide a diverse array of company statistical and security price information. For example, one can "screen" for companies that pass certain financial criteria, such as P/E ratio below 10 or debt-to-equity ratio under 50 percent. These services also contain detailed SEC filings and historical price data that cover tens of thousands of companies, and often provide over twenty years of data.

Putting all of this information into a software package, such as Equis's Metastock Professional, takes only a few keystrokes. In seconds such programs can generate charts that would have taken considerable time and effort if they had been painstakingly plotted by hand. These programs can also test trading strategies, examining how they would have responded on the basis of historical market data. Running a simulated strategy allows investors to test and fine-tune investment systems before risking real investment dollars.

Computers have opened up the area of technical analysis to many individuals. With a computer, technical analysis can be timely and tailored to an individual investment perspective.

For a more detailed examination of how computers can assist investors, consult *The Individual Investor's Guide to Computerized Investing* (available through the American Association of Individual Investors), listed in this book's Appendix.

CONCLUSION

Technical analysis focuses on the qualitative factors of trading. It is a general term used to refer to any sort of analysis that studies past price and volume trends, as well as other market-related indicators, to discover patterns that might be applied to forecast future price movements. Technical analysts exclude practically all of the information used by the fundamental analyst.

Technical analysis provides investors an additional source of information and another set of tools to use when making investment decisions.

Some investors will use technical analysis exclusively in making buy-sell decisions. Others will select likely securities using fundamental analysis and then use technical analysis to help determine entry and exit points. Even the most strict fundamental analysts may use technical analysis, if only to understand what is driving other investors.

5 / PORTFOLIO PERFORMANCE BENCHMARKS

OVERVIEW

Analysts investing in companies need benchmarks to gauge the overall performance of the securities markets, and of the securities they own. Averages and indices are measures that represent the general tone and direction of the market and of specific subsets of the market. Specialized averages and indices allow investors to gauge the performance of a variety of securities and portfolios that do not follow the trend of the overall market, but rather follow specific groups of securities. When examining performance it is important to select an index that matches the composition of the specific portfolio being compared. For example, an investor with a stock portfolio composed of well-established firms listed on the NYSE would compare portfolio performance against the Dow Jones Industrial Average. The Dow Jones Utility Average would be used as the benchmark if firms held were industry specific. A portfolio composed of smaller capitalization, over-the-counter stocks would be compared against the NASDAQ composite. Analysts should compare measures that represent similar securities.

AVERAGES AND INDICES

The primary difference between an index and an average is that an *average* is usually based on a small number of securities using a simple averaging method, whereas an *index* is usually based on a large number of securities. Further, most indices are set to a base, such as 100 points, as of a certain date, and changes are reflected and reported as changes in this base figure.

Two primary methods used in calculating averages and indices are: (1) summing the market value of the selected stocks and dividing by the number of issues and, (2) summing the market value of the selected stocks and dividing by a divisor that makes allowance for stock splits or other changes in capitalization.

The Dow Jones Averages

Dow Jones & Company, the publisher of *The Wall Street Journal*, publishes the Dow Jones averages. There are four separate averages, each based on a different subset of NYSE-listed securities—the *Industrial Average*, based on thirty large industrial companies; the *Transportation Average*, based on twenty large transportation companies (prior to 1970, it was known as the Railroad Index because it included only railroads); the *Utility Average*, based on fifteen large utility companies; and the *Composite Average*, based on all sixty-five stocks that comprise the other three averages. All four averages are expressed in points, not dollars.

The Dow Jones Industrial Average is the most commonly used measure of stock market performance. Its daily close is frequently quoted in television newscasts and local and national newspapers. This average is often criticized for representing too few stocks. However, the thirty stocks in the average make up about 15 to 20 percent of the total market value of all stocks listed on the New York Stock Exchange. (Here, market value is defined as the price times the number of shares outstanding for each company listed.)

The Dow Jones averages are price-weighted, which means that stocks with higher prices influence the movement of the index more than lower-priced stocks. A price-weighted, or un-weighted, average is computed by adding the prices of the stocks that compose the average (the numerator), and dividing by the number of stocks in the average (the divisor). For example, if a price-weighted average consisted of four stocks priced at 10, 20, 60 and 110 dollars per share, the index value would be 50—(10 + 20 + 60 + 110)/4. With this example it is easy to see how price movements of the higher-priced stock will move the average more than will a lower-priced stock. If the security priced at $110 moves up 10 percent, it will move the average up to 52.75—(10 + 20 + 60 + 121)/4—a change of 5.5 percent. However, if the $10 security increases by 10 percent, the average will increase only to 50.25—(11 + 20 + 60 + 110)/4—a change of just 0.5 percent.

Over time, the divisor for each of the Dow Jones averages is adjusted, although only downward, for stock splits and stock dividends that are equal to 10 percent (or 5 points) or more of the market value of a stock. When the Dow Jones Industrial Average was first computed, its divisor was 30—the number of stocks that made up the average. It is now just over 1.

Even with the potential problems of using such an un-weighted average, composed of a relatively small number of stocks, the Dow Jones averages seem to closely follow the trend of the market. This is probably because the securities in the average represent such a large portion of the market's capitalization.

Standard & Poor's Index

Standard & Poor's publishes five separate indices that are more broadly based than the Dow Jones averages. Each is based on a different subset of securities, most of which are traded on the New York Stock Exchange. The S&P *400 Industrial Index* is based on four hundred large industrial companies; the *20 Transportation Index* is based on twenty large transportation companies; the *40 Utility Index* is based on forty large utility companies; the *40 Financial Index* is based on forty large financial service companies; and the *500 Index* is based on all five hundred stocks that comprise the other four indices. All five indices are expressed in points.

These indices are constructed in a value- or capital-weighted fashion—the price of each stock is multiplied by its number of listed shares. Stocks that have greater total market value (price multiplied by total shares outstanding) influence the movement of the index more than smaller-market capitalization stocks. The weight assigned to each stock in the index is determined by the percentage of the stock's market value to the total market value of the stocks in the index. Consider the example in Table 5.1.

Table 5.1

Price Per Share ($)	Shares	Market Value	Index Weights (%)
10	1,500	15,000	41
20	300	6,000	16
60	150	9,000	25
110	60	6,600	18
		36,600	100

In this example, the $10 security (which makes up 41 percent of the index value) has a much greater influence in a value-weighted index than it would in a price-weighted index. Further, no problems result from adjusting the index for stock dividends and splits because the stock price will decrease in proportion to the increase in the number of shares outstanding, thus, mathematically cancelling the effect.

The value-weighted S&P indices are thought to better represent the whole market's performance than do the Dow Jones Averages. For one reason, the stocks in the S&P 500 represent over 80 percent of the total market capitalization of the stocks listed on the New York Stock Exchange. This is important to note when comparing how a portfolio of diversified, blue-chip stocks performs, and in computing risk statistics such as *beta*.

The S&P indices, although less closely followed by the general press, are widely available in financial newspapers such as *The Wall Street Journal, Barron's,* and *Investor's Daily.*

The New York Stock Exchange Indices (Composite Index)

The New York Stock Exchange indices are comprised of five separate indices, each based on a different subset of NYSE securities. Each one of the 1,500 stocks that make up the exchange is classified into one of four industry groups: *industrials, transportations, utilities*, and *financials*. The *composite* comprises all the stocks making up the other four groups, thereby representing the market as a whole. The composite index is quoted in dollars and cents, and the other four indices are shown only in point movements. The base for all five indices was originally set to a value of 50 points at the close of the market on December 31, 1965. Its current value reflects the appropriate changes in the market since that time.

These indices, calculated and printed on the tape every half hour, reflect the combined market value change in their component issues. Similar to the S&P Indices, each NYSE index is calculated in the value-weighted fashion.

The American Stock Exchange Market Value Index

The American Stock Exchange market value index is based on all common stocks and warrants traded on the AMEX. The index is value-weighted and is expressed in dollars and cents. The divisor of the AMEX index is also adjusted as new listings are added and old ones deleted. It is reported by the AMEX every half hour. The index was introduced in September 1973, with a base price of $100. In July 1983, the index was adjusted to half ($50) of the original level.

One feature that sets AMEX market value index apart from the others is that cash dividends paid by component stocks are assumed to be reinvested and are reflected in the index. This eases the process of comparing the total return (change in price plus dividends) of a portfolio. With other indices, the cash dividends paid out by the companies must be added back to the index, and the proper weighting factors must be applied, making such a calculation a monumental task.

The NASDAQ-OTC Price Indices

The NASDAQ-OTC price indices consist of seven value-weighted indices, each based on a different subset of NASDAQ securities. All domestic common stocks traded on NASDAQ are classified into one of six industry groups: *industrials, banks, insurance, transportation, utilities,* and *other financials.* The *composite* represents all stocks included in the other six groups, a total of about 3,500 companies. Each index is adjusted for all changes in capitalization, as well as for any domestic additions or deletions to NASDAQ. All seven indices, expressed in points, were originally set to a value of 100 at the close of the market on February 5, 1971. The NASDAQ-OTC price indices are important benchmarks for investors investing primarily in smaller companies that are not tracked by some of the blue chip-based indices.

The Value Line Composite Index

The Value Line average is comprised of 1,700 actively traded stocks listed on various exchanges that are regularly reviewed by the *Value Line Investment Survey.* Value Line covers a diverse cross-section of both small and large capitalization stocks. The index is expressed in points and computed using an equal-weighting system. All 1,700 stocks are weighted equally regardless of price or total market value. This is done by assuming that an equal amount is invested in every stock, a method that more closely resembles the method individuals use to balance personal portfolios. The index is adjusted for changes in capitalization, as well as for any additions and deletions to the *Value Line* list of stocks.

The index is a good resource for investors because of the weighting process used and diversity of companies covered by the *Value Line Investment Survey.*

CONCLUSION

The stock market averages and indices discussed here are considered to be the most widely used. Other indicators available to investors include Moody's Industrial Average, Moody's Railroad Stock Average, Wilshire 5,000, and Barron's 50-Stock Average. Investors wanting to know only if the market has moved up or down can look at any of these major market or broad based indicators. Those investors wishing to compare portfolio performance should choose an indicator more carefully.

Averages and indices help investors by determining the tone of the market and by providing benchmarks by which to judge performance. In examining various indices, it is important to remember how they are calculated and recognize potential distortions due to the weighting method used. In selecting an index, be sure to choose one that resembles the composition of the portfolio being tracked to avoid comparing apples and oranges. The indices presented are popular, so investors should have little trouble obtaining data. While local newspapers may not cover all the indices, any good financial newspaper (*The Wall Street Journal, Barron's,* or *Investor's Daily*) will provide detailed information. The diversity of averages and indices helps to ensure that a measure can be found that resembles the types of security or group of securities held by the investor.

APPENDIX / SOURCES
OF INFORMATION

ASSOCIATIONS

American Association of Individual Investors
625 North Michigan, Suite 1900
Chicago, IL 60615
(312)280-0170

With more than 100,000 members, this non-profit organization assists individuals to become effective managers of their own assets. AAII offers a monthly journal, educational materials, seminars, information services, and the annuals, *The Individual Investor's Guide to No-Load Mutual Funds* and *The Individual Investor's Guide to Computerized Investing*. All of the financial and investment database services mentioned in this book are listed and described in the *Guide to Computerized Investing*. The *Guide* also includes descriptions on over 380 investment software products.

National Association of Investors Corporation
1515 East Eleven Mile Road
Royal Oaks, MI 48067
(313)543-0612

A non-profit, volunteer organization of investors interested in sharing their experiences with others. Individual or investment club memberships available.

BUSINESS AND FINANCIAL PERIODICALS

Barron's
Dow Jones & Company
200 Burnett Road
Chicopee, MA 01020

A weekly newspaper that includes a wealth of statistical information about the stock market. In addition to publishing quotations on stocks, bonds, and options, the paper includes the advisory and investor sentiment readings.

Business Week
McGraw-Hill, Inc.
1221 Avenue of the Americas
New York, NY 10020

Weekly publication covering topics about specific companies and industries as well as general business-related subjects.

Changing Times
The Kiplinger Washington Editors, Inc.
Editors Park, MD 20782

Monthly magazine covering a range of pertinent and timely information—from investments and taxes to education and careers.

Financial World
Financial World Partners
P.O. Box 7098
Red Oak, IA 51591

Biweekly publication covering business, economic, and financial topics. Special features include management performance of major U.S. companies; analysis of stock, bond and mutual fund activity; and analysis of emerging companies and industries.

Forbes
Forbes, Inc.
60 Fifth Avenue
New York, NY 10011

Biweekly publication includes articles and commentaries on many companies, industries, and personalities. Special annual issues include: mutual fund ranking by market performance, and a listing of the largest corporations by revenue, profitability, growth, and market performance.

Fortune
Time & Life Building
Rockefeller Center
New York, NY 10020

Biweekly publication includes in-depth discussion on particular companies and industries, the economy, and investing. Special issues list the 500 largest U.S. corporations, and the 50 largest companies by industry.

Investor's Daily
1941 Armacost Avenue
Los Angeles, CA 90025

Daily newspaper covers topics on all business and investment related topics. In addition to stock market statistical information, also measures companies' EPS growth in the last five years, each stock's relative daily price change over the last twelve months, and the stock's trading volume in terms of its change above or below the stock's average daily volume.

The Media General Financial Weekly
P.O. Box C-32333
Richmond, VA 23293

Weekly publication includes a broad range of market opinions and a vast amount of market statistical information.

The New York Times
229 West 43rd Street
New York, NY 10036

Daily publication covering comprehensive business and financial-related topics.

The Wall Street Journal
Dow Jones & Company
200 Barnett Road
Chicopee, MA 01020

Published Monday through Friday, includes comprehensive coverage of current business, financial, economic, industry, and international news.

EXCHANGES

All exchanges should have available detailed brochures explaining how each exchange works and how the securities and commodities are traded, as well as current listings of securities/commodities traded:

American Stock Exchange
86 Trinity Place
New York, NY 10006
(212)306-1000

Chicago Board of Trade
141 West Jackson
Chicago, IL 60604
(312)435-3500

Chicago Board Options Exchange
400 South LaSalle
Chicago, IL 60605
(312)786-5600

Commodity Exchange, Inc. (COMEX)
4 World Trade Center
New York, NY 10048
(212)938-2900

Kansas City Board of Trade
4800 Main Street, Suite 303
Kansas City, MO 64112
(816)753-7500

MidAmerica Commodity Exchange
444 West Jackson
Chicago, IL 60606
(312)341-3000

Midwest Stock Exchange
440 South LaSalle
Chicago, IL 60605
(312)663-2222

New York Futures Exchange
20 Broad Street
New York, NY 10005
(212)656-4949
(800)221-7722

New York Mercantile Exchange
4 World Trade Center
New York, NY 10048
(212)938-2222

New York Stock Exchange
11 Wall Street
New York, NY 10005
(212)656-3000

Pacific Stock Exchange
301 Pine Street
San Francisco, CA 94104
(415)393-4000

Philadelphia Stock Exchange
Philadelphia Board of Trade
1900 Market Street
Philadelphia, PA 19103
(215)496-5000

FEDERAL RESERVE BANKS

There are twelve Federal Reserve Banks. The St. Louis Branch is especially helpful with its publications, *U.S. Financial Data*, a weekly analysis of current interest rates and money market conditions, and *National Economic Trends*, a monthly covering the national business situation. Other Federal Reserve publications are available by writing to specific Federal Reserve Banks. In addition, Federal Reserve banks can be contacted to purchase U.S. Government securities without incurring any brokerage costs.

Federal Reserve Bank of
Atlanta
104 Marietta Street, N.W.
Atlanta, GA 30303
(404)521-8500

Federal Reserve Bank
of Boston
600 Atlantic Avenue
Boston, MA 02106
(617)973-3000

Federal Reserve Bank of
Chicago
230 South LaSalle Street
Chicago, IL 60690
(312)322-5322

Federal Reserve Bank
of Cleveland
1455 East Sixth Street
Cleveland, OH 44114
(216)579-2000

Federal Reserve Bank of
Dallas
400 South Akard
Dallas, TX 75202
(214)651-6111

Federal Reserve Bank
of Kansas City
925 Grand Avenue
Kansas City, MO 64198
(816)881-2000

Federal Reserve Bank
of Minneapolis
250 Marquette Avenue
Minneapolis, MN 55480
(612)340-2345

Federal Reserve Bank
of New York
33 Liberty Street
New York, NY 10045
(212)720-5000

Federal Reserve Bank
of Philadelphia
10 Independence Mall
Philadelphia, PA 19106
(215)574-6000

Federal Reserve Bank
of Richmond
701 East Byrd Street
Richmond, VA 23219
(804)697-8000

Federal Reserve Bank
of St. Louis
411 Locust Street
St. Louis, MO 63102
(314)444-8444

Federal Reserve Bank
of San Francisco
101 Market Street
San Francisco, CA 94105
(415)974-2000

GOVERNMENT SOURCES

The U.S. Government compiles a lot of economic, corporate, and
industry data. A complete listing of all publications, including the
ones described here, are available from the Superintendent of

Documents. Following are descriptions of a few that are pertinent to the subject covered in this text.

Superintendent of Documents
Government Printing Office
Washington, D.C. 20402

Business Conditions Digest (BCD)

A monthly publication available by subscription from the Bureau of Economic Analysis. A composite index compiled from the 12 leading economic indicators.

Economic Indicators

A monthly publication published by the U.S. Council of Economic Advisors contains summaries on many aspects of the economy, including spending, industrial production, prices, money, federal finance, and credit.

Federal Reserve Bulletin

Published monthly by the Board of Governors of the Federal Reserve System, contains a lot of data on the monetary situation.

Survey of Current Business

A publication from the U.S. Department of Commerce. Weekly supplements include articles, economic statistics, and data on industries and finance.

U.S. Industrial Outlook

Published annually by the U.S. Department of Commerce. Periodic economic censuses on the construction, manufacturing, mineral, and selected service industries; the retail and wholesale trades; and transportation.

INDEXING SERVICES

Funk and Scott Index of Corporations and Industries
Predicast, Inc.
11001 Cedar Street
Cleveland, OH 44141
(800)321-6388
(216)795-3000

Indexes articles about companies, industries, and products from over 750 financial publications. Groups of related products are classified by the Standard Classification (SIC) code, a product classification system.

Business Periodicals Index
H.W. Wilson Co.
950 University Avenue
Bronx, NY 10452
(212)588-8400

Indexes articles about companies and industries published by major business periodicals.

MAJOR FINANCIAL SERVICES ORGANIZATIONS

Standard & Poor's Corporation
345 Hudson Street
New York, NY 10014
(212)208-1004

Offers numerous financial services including S&P's Daily News Section, Corporation Records, Industry Surveys, Stock and Bond Guides, NYSE and OTC Stock Reports, and Trendline.

Moody's Investor Service
99 Church Street
New York, NY 10007
(212)553-0300

Offers many financial services including Moody's Industrial Manual, OTC Industrial Manual, Bank & Financial Manual, Public Utility Manual, Transportation Manual, Municipal & Government Manual, and Handbook of Widely Held Common Stocks.

The Value Line Investment Survey
Value Line, Inc.
711 Third Avenue
New York, NY 10017
(212)687-3965
(800)634-3583

Examines a broad field of 1,700 stocks each week. Up-to-date information in three sections: Selection & Opinion contains articles and computer screens on investment ideas that merit special attention along with Value Line's views on financial markets, the economy, and other matters of public interest; Summary & Index shows the updated ratings of 1,700 stocks for future relative performance and safety; and in Ratings & Reports, each of 1,700 stocks is the subject of a comprehensive new full-page rating and report at least once every three months.

NEWSLETTERS

Rather than list the hundreds of available investment newsletters, the following key guides are recommended to begin investigating newsletter options.

Individual Investor's Guide to Investment Publications
International Publishing Corporation
P.O. Box 11087
Chicago, IL 60615
(312)943-7354

A comprehensive sourcebook listing names and addresses of over 1,500 investment newsletters, including full descriptions (editor, background, editorial direction, prices) on over 600 publications. Organized by 24 investment categories (stocks, bonds, mutual funds, commodities, international investing, etc.).

The Hulbert Guide to Financial Newsletters
Probus Publishing
118 North Clinton Street
Chicago, IL 60606
(312)346-7985

Monitors and ranks the performance of more than 100 investment newsletters.

OTHER SOURCES MENTIONED

Nelson's Directory of Investment Research
Nelson Publications
P.O. Box 591
Port Chester, NY 10573
(914)937-8400

The directory lists analysts and specialty subjects researched. Includes top corporate officers and the names of the brokerage houses researching specific firms.

Vickers Weekly Insider Report
Vickers Stock Research Corporation
226 New York Avenue
Huntington, NY 11743
(516)423-7710

Contains every open market trade of more than 500 shares, and rates each stock according to insider activity; lists 10 top stocks and 10 least liked stocks; compares insider trading ratio (S/B) with Dow Industrials every week; treasury acquisitions; breakdown by industry. Every new subscriber receives insider trading formula that has beaten the Dow Jones Industrial average by +200% since 1972.

GLOSSARY

Agency trade: A security transaction involving a customer and a broker who is transacting business on behalf of the customer and charging a commission for the service.

Agent: One who acts on behalf of others, not incurring any risk in the process.

American Stock Exchange (AMEX or ASE): The second largest securities exchange in the United States. The exchange, located in Manhattan, contains primarily small- to medium-size companies, especially energy securities.

Ask (offer): The lowest price anyone has offered to accept for a security at a given time.

Assets: Items of value owned by a company such as cash, accounts receivable, inventory, and plant and equipment.

Back office: The transaction processing department of a brokerage firm.

Balance sheet: A statement showing the status of a company's assets, liabilities, and shareholders' equity at a given point in time.

Bearer bond: A bond that is not registered in a specific name, but is payable to the holder.

Bear market: A market trend in which security prices are generally falling.

Best-efforts offering: An arrangement by an investment banker to sell a security for a company while acting as an agent of the company. The investment banker does not buy the issue outright to resell to the market, but does make its "best effort" to sell the issue.

Beta: A measure of risk and return, with 1 being equal to the market.

Bid: The highest price anyone has offered to pay for a security at a given time.

Big Board: Another name for the New York Stock Exchange.

Blue chip: The stock of a company that has earned a reputation for quality products and services and for its consistent ability to make money for shareholders.

Bond: An IOU or promissory note of a company, typically issued in $1,000 increments, carrying a specified interest rate and maturing on a specified date.

Bondholder: The owner of a bond, that is, a party who has loaned money to a bond issuer.

Book value: The net worth of a company as determined by an accounting calculation in which the intangible assets, current liabilities, and long-term liabilities are subtracted from total assets. Some reporting services, however, do not net out intangibles while computing book value.

Breakout: A distinct price movement made by a security after trading for a period of time in a consolidation pattern.

Broker (also Brokerage firm): An organization, licensed by the Securities and Exchange Commission, that acts as an agent to negotiate the purchase and sale of securities for others, charging commissions for this service.

Broker loan rate (or Call money rate): The interest rate charged on loans to brokers on stock exchange collateral.

Bull market: A market trend in which security prices are generally rising.

Callable security: A security which, at the option of the issuer and as determined by a specified set of conditions, can be redeemed in whole or in part.

Call option: The right to buy a stock at a specified price by a specified date.

Capital gain: The profit calculated when a security is sold for more than its purchase price.

Capital loss: The loss calculated when a security is sold for less than its purchase price.

Capital structure: A company's financial framework, which includes its long-term debt, preferred stock, and shareholders' equity. It does not include short-term liabilities.

Capital surplus: Shareholders' equity representing the amount of money received, above the par value of common stock, when it is issued by the company.

Cash sale (or Same day): A transaction that settles the same day as the trade occurs.

Clearing: The process of comparing a security transaction and freeing it and its associated payment from obligation.

Clearing corporation: An organization that specializes in clearing the security transactions of its members.

Clearing member: A brokerage firm that holds a membership in, and is therefore entitled to use the services of, one of the nation's clearing corporations.

Collateral: Property pledged by a borrower to secure a loan.

Common dividend: A payment made from retained earnings to common stock shareholders; paid after preferred dividends.

Common stock: A security that represents a share of the common ownership in a corporation and has no preferential claims to income or assets.

Contrabroker: The brokerage firm on the other side of a security transaction.

Corporation account: A brokerage account opened by a corporation.

Correspondent: A brokerage firm that performs services for another brokerage firm.

Cost of capital: The rate of return a company is required to pay for the use of capital.

Cost of goods sold (or Cost of sales): The cost of the inventory sold.

Current asset: An asset owned by a company that can be converted into cash in a relatively short period of time.

Current liability: Money owed by a company that must be paid within one year.

Current yield: The cash return a security pays divided by the price of the security.

Custodian account: A brokerage account opened by a person of legal age for the benefit of someone who is not of legal age.

Day order: An order to buy or sell a security that expires at the end of the same trading day if it has not been executed.

Dealer: An organization, licensed by the Securities and Exchange Commission, that, acting in a principal capacity, buys securities, marks them up, and then resells them.

Debenture: A promissory note backed by the general credit of a company, rather than by any specific collateral.

Debt: An obligation of a company such as accounts payable, notes payable, taxes payable, deferred taxes, and long-term debt.

Debt security: A security depicting money borrowed that must be repaid by a specific time and that carries a stated interest rate.

Default: The failure to pay interest or principal when due.

Depository Trust Company (DTC): A central securities certificate depository that members of a clearing corporation use to hold their securities, thus facilitating the use of the clearing corporation's computerized bookkeeping system. This system is a faster, more economical way to process securities transactions than the process of physically delivering, receiving, and exchanging money.

Depreciation: The amortization of an asset's cost, less its salvage value, over the life of the asset. It is an accounting process that has the effect of reducing the taxable income of a company, but not its cash flow.

Discretionary account: An account in which someone other than the account holder has the right and responsibility to make purchase and sale decisions.

Dividend: A payment made, out of the retained earnings, to the stockholders of a company.

Dividend yield: The dividend of a stock divided by its market price.

Du Pont analysis: A method of financial ratio analysis that illustrates how efficient company operations and proper use of financing affect return on equity. The analysis shows the relationship and interaction between the various financial ratios. The process is named for the Du Pont Corporation, which developed this analytical technique.

Earnings before interest and taxes (EBIT or Income before interest and taxes): The income generated by a company from all sources, less all the expenses associated with generating this income, with the exception of interest charges, taxes, and extraordinary items.

Earnings statement (or Income statement): A statement issued by a company showing its earnings or losses over a given period.

Equity: The ownership interest maintained by shareholders in a company, calculated by subtracting total liabilities from total assets.

Equity security: An instrument that represents ownership interest in a company.

Ex-dividend: A security without rights to an upcoming dividend distribution.

Ex-dividend date: The day on which a security begins trading in the open market on an ex-dividend basis, normally the fourth business day prior to the record date.

Execution: The transaction of an order to buy or sell a security.

Ex-rights: Without right—shares that are trading ex-rights are trading without the right to subscribe to a new issue of stock that is offered to existing shareholders of a company.

Fiduciary account: A brokerage account opened by an executor, administrator, trustee, guardian, conservator, or committee that has been duly appointed to represent those parties concerned with the assets held in an account.

Fixed asset: A physical asset—such as property or plant and equipment—used by a company in its operations, not expected to be converted into cash within the current year.

Fixed charge: A contractual payment on long-term leased goods and interest on long-term debt, such as machines, property, and liabilities.

Flag: A consolidation pattern that indicates a trend will continue, formed after a dynamic, nearly straight move in a market.

Floor broker (or **Two-dollar broker**): A member of a stock exchange who executes buy or sell orders on the floor of the exchange.

Gap: A "hole" occurring in the orderly trading of a stock, when the highest price on one day is lower than the lowest price the next day or when the lowest price one day is higher than the highest price the next day.

Good Until Canceled order (GTC order or **Open order):** An order to buy or sell a security that remains in effect until it is either executed or canceled.

Gross sales: The total sales at the billed price, not adjusted for discounts, returns or allowances, or other adjustments.

Growth stock: The stock of a company whose earnings have grown or are expected to grow rapidly.

Income statement (Earnings statement or Statement of operations): A statement issued by a company showing its earnings or losses over a given period.

Individual account: A brokerage account opened by an individual investor.

Initial public offering (IPO): A company's first selling of its stock to the general public.

Intangible asset: An asset with an actual value that is difficult or impossible to determine, such as patents and trademarks.

Interest: The charge paid by a borrower to a lender for the use of money. It is expressed as a rate for a specific period of time, usually one year.

Investment club: Individuals who have pooled their funds for the purpose of investing.

Investment club account: A brokerage account opened by an investment club.

Joint account: A brokerage account opened by two or more individuals.

Joint tenants account: A joint account wherein, upon the death of one tenant, the property in the account passes to the surviving tenant.

Leverage: The use of borrowed money to magnify a company's return on assets.

Liability: A claim against the assets of a company.

Limit order: An order to buy or sell a stated amount of a security at a specified price that can only fill at that price or a more advantageous one.

Liquidity: The ease and rapidity with which assets can be converted into cash.

Liquid market: The ability of a market to absorb a reasonable amount of buying or selling without the market price being inflated or depressed excessively.

Long: A term signifying ownership of securities.

Long-term: A term used to classify assets that will be used longer than one year or liability that will not be repaid in one year.

Margin account: A brokerage account that includes a line of credit that can be used for anything, as regulated by the Federal Reserve's Regulation T.

Margin call: A demand on a margin customer to add money or securities to the account so that the line of credit remains properly secured with respect to federal regulations (Regulation T).

Market order: An order to buy or sell a security at the best price obtainable on the market immediately upon the order reaching the floor of the exchange.

Market price (Price quote, Quotation, or Quote): The last price at which a security was trading, determined by the forces of supply and demand.

Market Value: The price of a security which is indicated by the last recorded trade.

Member: An individual who owns a seat on a stock exchange.

Member firm: An organization that has an officer, partner, or principal who is a member of a stock exchange.

Midwest Stock Exchange (MSE): One of the largest securities exchanges in the United States. Located in Chicago.

Momentum: The rate of change in a price, or volume movement.

Multiple: (See Price-Earnings ratio or P/E ratio.)

Municipal bond: A bond, issued by a state or municipal government, that pays interest generally free from Federal income tax.

National Association of Securities Dealers (NASD): The self-regulating association of the broker/dealer industry that sets and enforces rules of fair practice for the securities industry and whose primary purpose is to protect investors who deal in the over-the-counter market.

National Association of Securities Dealers Automated Quotations system (NASDAQ): A computerized system that provides securities quotations on the OTC stocks. NASDAQ is owned and operated by the NASD.

National Market Exchange (NME): An electronic link that ties together some of the largest over-the-counter dealers in the United States, thereby creating a kind of pseudo-exchange for the transaction of over-the-counter securities.

Net accounts receivables: Accounts receivables adjusted for bad debt.

Net assets: The difference between total assets and total liabilities.

Net income: The difference between gross sales revenue and all company costs and expenses.

Net sales: Gross sales less any discounts, returns or allowances, or other adjustments.

New York Stock Exchange (NYSE or Big Board): The oldest and largest securities exchange in the United States. Founded in 1792, it is located at 11 Wall Street, New York. Over 1,600 companies are listed on the New York Stock Exchange, which has stringent listing requirements.

Next day: A transaction that settles on the first business day following the trade date.

Nonclearing member: A brokerage firm that is not a member of any clearing corporation and therefore must clear security transactions by physically moving certificates and money through the postal service or other couriers.

Odd lot: A quantity of stock that is less than a round lot; that is, less than 100 shares for actively traded stocks and less than 10 shares for inactively traded ones.

Offer (Ask): The lowest price anyone has offered to accept for a security at a given time.

Option: A contract that gives the holder the right to buy or sell a stated amount of a stock (usually 100 shares) at a specified price within a specified time.

Overbought market: A condition in which the market, having moved up so quickly, has used up much of the buying volume normally overhanging the market and is due for a pullback.

Oversold market: A condition in which the market, having moved down so quickly, has used up much of the selling volume normally overhanging the market and is due for a rally.

Over-the-Counter market (OTC market): A securities market in which transactions occur through a network of telephones and computers instead of through physical floor exchange.

Over-the-Counter Security (OTC security): A security that is not listed or traded on an organized securities exchange.

Pacific Stock Exchange (PSE): One of the largest regional securities exchanges in the United States. The PSE opens at the same time as the NYSE and closes one-half hour later.

Paid-in capital: (See Capital Surplus.)

Partnership account: A brokerage account opened by a partnership, requiring the signatures of all of the general partners, and also requiring a copy of the partnership agreement.

Payment date: The date on which a corporation actually makes the distribution to the list of individuals who are entitled to receive it as per the record date.

Pennant: A consolidation pattern, formed after a dynamic and nearly straight move in a market, that indicates a trend will continue.

Portfolio: The complete investment holdings of an individual or institution.

Preferred dividend: Dividend payments made to preferred stockholders. Preferred dividends have a specified rate and must be paid before common dividends can be paid.

Preferred stock: A security that represents a share of preferred ownership in a corporation, having preferential claims to income or assets over those claims held by common stock.

Price-Earnings ratio (or P/E ratio or Multiple): The market price of a stock divided by its annual earnings per share.

Principal trade: A security transaction involving a customer and a dealer who is working from inventory, wherein no commissions are charged but a markup is earned on the inventory position.

Profit taking: The act of realizing a profit by closing out a security position.

Pullback: A brief decline in prices occurring after a major move up.

Put option: The right to sell a stock at a specified price by a specified date.

Rally: A brief rise in prices occurring after a major market decline.

Random-Walk Theory: A theory stating that stock prices change in a random fashion, so that past prices have no impact on and are of no use in predicting future prices.

Record date: The date on which a corporation closes its list of security holders to determine who is entitled to receive a distribution or proxy solicitation.

Rectangle: A consolidation pattern formed as a result of a battle between two groups over-hanging the market at different fixed prices.

Registered representative: An individual who works for a brokerage firm and is properly licensed to serve the investing public.

Regulation T: A Federal Reserve regulation that governs the amount of credit brokers can advance to customers who are buying securities on margin.

Regulation U: A Federal Reserve regulation that governs the amount of credit banks can advance to customers buying securities on margin.

Resistance level: A price level that temporarily halts an upward movement in a stock's price.

Retained earnings (undistributed profits or earned surplus): The earnings kept after dividends have been paid which increase shareholder equity in a company.

Reverse split: The division of the outstanding shares of a stock into a smaller number of shares.

Round lot: The most common unity in which securities are traded, typically 100 shares for actively traded stocks and 10 shares for inactively traded ones.

Seat: A membership on a securities exchange.

Securities Investor Protection Corporation (SIPC): A government-sponsored private corporation that protects brokerage customer accounts.

Security: An investment instrument such as a stock, bond, option, or warrant.

Settlement date: The day on which a security transaction is actually settled (securities and money are exchanged).

Shareholder equity: The calculation of a company's total assets minus its total liabilities.

Short position: The ownership position in a security after a short sale has been made but before the position has been covered.

Short selling: The act of selling a security that is not currently owned, with the intention of buying it back at a cheaper price at some future point in time.

Short-term: A term used to classify assets that will be used within one year or liabilities that will be repaid within one year.

Specialist: A member of a stock exchange appointed by the exchange and charged with the responsibility of maintaining an orderly succession of prices for a specific security trading on the exchange.

Split: The division of the outstanding shares of a stock into a larger number of shares.

Start-up (seed) money: The first monetary contribution toward the financing of a new organization.

Stock: A security that represents a share of ownership in a corporation.

Stock dividend: A dividend paid in additional shares of stock instead of in cash.

Stockholder (or Shareholder): The owner of at least one share of stock in a corporation.

Stockholder of record: A stockholder whose name is registered on the books of the issuing corporation and therefore is entitled to receive the distribution.

Stock market (Securities exchange or Stock exchange): An organized market for buying and selling securities.

Stop limit order: An order to buy securities at a price above, or sell at a price below, the current market price, which becomes a limit order only when the security trades at or through that price.

Stop order: An order to buy securities at a price above, or sell at a price below, the current market price, which becomes a market order only when the security trades at or through that price.

Street name: A security held in the name of the brokerage firm instead of the name of the customer.

Support level: A price level that temporarily halts a downward movement in price.

Ticker symbol (or Stock symbol): The unique symbol used by brokers to represent a security. Consisting of one to five letters, it is assigned by the exchange on which the security trades, or by NASDAQ for securities that do not trade on exchanges.

Ticker tape (Ticker): The stream of securities transactions occurring on an exchange. The name is derived from the ticking noise that the original machines made as they printed trading information. The ticker tape contains information such as the ticker symbol, the class of security, last price, volume, and exchange on which the last trade occurred.

Trade date: The day on which a security transaction is executed.

Treasury bill (Treasuries or T-bill): A short-term security issued by the U.S. Treasury Department, in maturities of 91 days, 182 days, and 52 weeks. Backed by the full faith and credit of the U.S. government, these securities are often considered as being the closest item to a risk-free security.

Treasury stock: Stock reacquired by the issuing company that has been previously issued and outstanding, but is not currently outstanding.

Triangle: A consolidation pattern formed, resulting from an indecision on the part of buyers and sellers.

Warrant: A security that gives the holder the right to buy another security at a stipulated price for a specified or perpetual period of time.

When issued (or when, as, and if issued): A conditional transaction in an authorized, but not as yet issued, security.

Year-end inventory: The value of inventory owned by a company at the end of its fiscal year.

Yield: The cash return a security pays divided by the market price of the security.

Yield to maturity: The total return a bond will pay, including the yield and any gain or loss that will be realized upon maturity, computed so as to represent an annualized percentage.

INDEX

Triple bottom, 109
Triple top, 108-109

Unchanged issues index, 123

Value Line composite index,
133-134
*Value Line's Food Industry
Composite*, 94
Value Line Industry Survey, 89,
94
Value Line Investment Survey,
17, 88-89, 97, 133, 134

Value-weighted index,
131-132
Venture capital, 6
Vertical line chart, 104
Volume data, 101

Wall Street Journal (The), 18,
119, 120, 123, 125, 126, 127,
130
Warner Computer Systems, 127
Weighted moving average, 103
Wilshire 5,000, 134

Year-end inventory, 34